Everyday Something Has Tried to

Kill Me and Has Failed

Everyday Something Has Tried to Kill Me and Has Failed

KIM McLARIN

PUBLISHING

New York, NY

Ig Publishing
Box 2547
New York, NY 10163
www.igpub.com

ISBN: 978-1-63246-158-2

Lucille Clifton, "won't you celebrate with me" from *The Book of Light*. Copyright © 1993 by Lucille Clifton. Reprinted with the permission of The Permissions Company, LLC on behalf of Copper Canyon Press, coppercanyonpress.org.

"Run for your Life" was originally published in *The New England Review*, Vol 43. No 1. 2022.

"On White Violence, Black Survival, and Learning to Shoot" was originally published in *The Sun Magazine*, October 2021.

To Saint James, otherwise known as Uncle Jimmy, otherwise known as Mr. Baldwin. For showing the way.

won't you celebrate with me

won't you celebrate with me
what i have shaped into
a kind of life? i had no model.
born in babylon
both nonWhite and woman
what did i see to be except myself?
i made it up
here on this bridge between
starshine and clay,
my one hand holding tight
my other hand; come celebrate
with me that everyday
something has tried to kill me
and has failed.

—Lucille Clifton

Contents

PART ONE

This Stuff Again

On White Violence, Black Survival and Learning to Shoot

On the outside, the Weston Shooters Club is pretty much what I expected: a graceless gray warehouse tucked off the highway behind a gas station in a dumpy part of town. Inside, however, the club is surprisingly clubby: deep leather chairs, slate-gray floors, a wine bar glowing warmly in the incandescent light. There is an ammo vending machine, the first I have ever seen, tucked unobtrusively in a corner and a beautiful blue globe gleaming on an end table, as if waiting for the Great White Hunter to enter and give it a spin.

"This is the Cadillac of gun clubs," brags Jack, our instructor. There isn't, he says, another like it in Massachusetts.

Jack is small statured, silver-haired, and non-posturing, a man who does not strike me as a cop. This is a relief. When searching for a basic firearms-safety class, I'd purposefully avoided the one closest to our house because it was also near the state police headquarters. Its website bragged that most of the instructors were officers.

Once the rest of the group has arrived, Jack introduces himself: NRA-certified instructor, "shooting enthusiast," many years of teaching experience. Pointing to his American-flag neck gaiter, he says he has a hard time talking for four hours through a face covering. "Anybody going to freak out if I take it off every now and then?"

I raise an eyebrow but say nothing. It is January 2021, a full year into the pandemic; at this point who even has strength to complain? Anyway, his gaiter will do about as much good on his neck as it does on his face, so why insist he pull it up? The conference-room door is open; the club, I have been told, uses MERV 13 filters in its air system; and my husband and I have come prepared with N95 masks. I inch my chair away from Jack, and we go on.

Thanks to the pandemic, the class is small: just seven students. In addition to us there are: a married couple from Brookline in their thirties, two strapping young brothers barely out of their teens, and a thin young man who sits alone at the end of the table, dressed head-to-toe in black, including a hoodie. Mrs. Brookline is Asian. I am Black. Everyone else, including my husband, is White.

The basic firearms-safety course approved by the Commonwealth of Massachusetts requires only four hours of instruction. By comparison, a motorcycle license, which I obtained last year, requires fifteen hours of instruction over the course of two days, the bulk of which is operating the bike itself. The Commonwealth does not require live fire to be part of its basic firearms course. In Massachusetts you can get a license to carry a gun without ever touching a weapon, much less shooting one. Still, Jack assures us that, unlike some other, inferior, courses, ours will include the chance to actually shoot.

"I want this class to be fun," he says.

While Jack talks, I flip through the *NRA Guide to the Basics of Pistol Shooting*, a 150-page, spiral-bound textbook featuring many, many photographs of guns and people shooting them. A Smith & Wesson ad on the first page reads: "Congratulations on Becoming Part of the Firearms Community." The guide says that "Americans own pistols today for many different reasons. Some people compete in the various types of pistol shooting matches held throughout the country, including those held at the collegiate and Olympic level. Hunters, too, have found that the use of a pistol to take game can be a challenging and exciting experience, and nearly all of the fifty states allow pistol hunting. A new shooter will quickly discover that pistol shooting is fun!"

For the second time the word *fun* startles me, given the context. I did not come to a class about weapons expecting to have fun.

Jack asks us to go around the table and introduce ourselves, giving our history with firearms and our reason for taking the class. Unexpectedly he begins with me. The first part of the assignment is easy: I have never fired a gun, never held one, never wanted to do so. No paintball or air rifles, no water pistols since I was nine or ten. My family includes many veterans and at least one member of law enforcement, so legal gun ownership is not beyond my experience, but knowing there's a gun in the house makes me feel less safe, not more. Statistics back me up on this, but even if they didn't, it wouldn't matter, since feelings are what we're talking about. All safety is an illusion, said James Baldwin. It's just a matter of which illusion you pick.

My feelings about guns are wholly negative, a fact that causes me to stumble on the assignment's second part. The whole class waits while my mind races for a response. In truth I'm reluctant to say what has brought me to this place on a bitter January morning; reluctant to tell a room full of White people why a progressive, NRA-hating, middle-aged Black woman has decided, this late in life, to get a gun.

∼

What violence I saw as a child was enacted mostly by White people, in whose glowing, televised company I spent much of my time. From heroic cops like Kojak and Baretta, to heroic cowboys like those on *Bonanza*, to heroic freaks like the Bionic Woman and the Six Million Dollar Man, the White folks who strutted through our living room every evening were forever solving their problems with fists or feet or guns. Even the women on *Dynasty*, so rich they never wore the same dress twice, rolled around in the dirt smacking one another. My sisters and I never fought that aggressively. My mother would have had a fit.

By comparison the Black folks on television largely spent

their time helping or joking or making people laugh. On *Starsky & Hutch*, Huggy Bear was a hustler, but he never shot anybody. Fred Sanford was a grouch who aimed his stinging barbs only against other Black people. Freddie "Boom Boom" Washington on *Welcome Back, Kotter* was a slacker, but to solve problems he used his charm. Setting aside the Blaxploitation movies (which we were not allowed to watch) and the occasional Black actors who played law-enforcement officers, like Clarence Williams or Georg Stanford Brown, the Black folks who appeared on the screen were strikingly nonviolent. Even the enslaved people in *Roots* rarely fought back, preferring to outrun, outsmart, or endure. *Maybe* a little spit in massa's cup. Thus the message was absorbed long before it was understood: in America violence is for White people. The only acceptable stance for Black folks is nonresistant suffering.

I am not a violent person. I have never been in a fight, never hit someone, never been slapped or kicked or punched. The closest I've ever come to a physical altercation is getting in the face of a few White people: A woman who touched my hair. A repo man who kept showing up at my mother's house to harass her over a debt she didn't owe. (A relative had used her name to finance a car.) A man who asked, at a park near my house, if I "even lived in this town" after I asked him to pick up after his dog. A neighbor who called me "uppity." In these moments I stood up but did not strike out, restraining the urge toward violence not for their sake, but for my own. It is possible to be angry without being violent, especially if one lacks power. Especially if one is non-wealthy and female and Black.

It is also possible to be violent without being angry— just ask the cop who knelt so casually on George Floyd's neck. Not every person attacking the U.S. Capitol on January 6 was raging mad. See the people taking selfies in the hallways. See the insurrectionist leaders calmly carrying their zip ties and issuing instructions. See the hordes chatting gaily as they mill around their hangman's noose. Not everyone was angry that day, but everyone had power and knew it; it was precisely that power they were there to defend. Beforehand they flew across the country on private jets or rode on rented buses from suburban Boston, toasting and singing as they came. Afterward they sat around in hotel lobbies, drinking beer and jovially recounting their experiences.

For all the lies about the Black Lives Matter protests—and about the Civil Rights Movement protests before them, and the anti-lynching crusades before that, and the Red Summer before that, and the abolitionist writings before that—the simple truth is that Black people in America have never been as violent toward White people as White people have been toward us, and that White violence against Black people is usually calculated. A friend of mine gasped reading that statement, but the only surprising thing about it is that anyone, knowing history, should be surprised. Consider the incalculable violence of 250 years of slavery. Consider the bloody rise of the KKK.

Consider the nearly 4,500 lynchings of Black people by White people documented by the Equal Justice Initiative, and the thousands more yet to be documented. Consider Tulsa in 1921 and New York in 1863 and Memphis and New Orleans in 1866 and Wilmington in 1898 and Atlanta in 1906 and Springfield in 1908 and East St. Louis in 1917 and Chicago in 1919 and Rosewood in 1923. Consider Ida B. Wells's groundbreaking book, *The Red Record*, in which she documented the true causes of lynchings and anti-Black violence during the Jim Crow era as overwhelmingly economic. Consider, as just one example, the Elaine Massacre, which took place in Elaine, Arkansas, during the Red Summer of 1919: White mobs slaughtered between fifty and one hundred Black sharecroppers who had asked for a better share of the profits from their labor. Consider Fred Hampton and Mark Clark and Medgar Evers and Dr. King.

Conservatives love to decry the violence of Black uprisings like those of the Long, Hot Summer of 1967, or those following the 1992 acquittal of the police who beat Rodney King, or the Black Lives Matter protests of 2020, without ever mentioning the relentless White violence that ignited them. But even in those uprisings it is inevitably Black people who bear the brunt of the violence. The 1967 riots, largely sparked by police beatings and shootings of unarmed Black men, left between eighty and one hundred people dead, the vast majority of them Black and a large portion killed by cops. No one knows the number of Black men killed by police in the years *preceding* either those uprisings or more recent ones. Though organizations such as Mapping Police Violence have been trying to subvert governmental unwillingness to track this public-health data by doing it themselves, such efforts go back only a few years. The true toll of decades and decades of police violence against Black people remains as much a mystery as the number of Black lives lost to lynching and White mob violence.

But some things are clear: Power begets violence. Violence reinforces power. White Americans damn well know this much.

Why are you here? This is the question Jack has asked me in front of the group. *Why do you want a gun?*

I try to dodge the question. "I'm . . . interested in things," I say.

"Interested?"

"I'm a writer."

"A writer! I hope you aren't going to write about me!" Jack says with a grin.

A lot of people say this when I tell them what I do for a living—or, rather, a lot of *men* say this. Men assume you want to write about them, whether or not that is true. I have learned to ignore the response. Instead I explain that I'm simply curious about the experience, that I am curious about many things.

"Last year I was curious about motorcycles," I say. "I got my license."

"Motorcycles!" Jack laughs. "A lot more dangerous than shooting!"

Motorcycles are indeed dangerous. When my husband first told me he intended to purchase one, after having given up riding for twenty years while raising his kids, I was nervous. But, for the record, more than 19,000 Americans were killed in gun-related violence in 2020, compared to roughly 5,000 annual motorcycle fatalities. Motorcycles are dangerous, but motorcycles are made for transportation. Guns are made to kill.

After I am done, my husband shares his history (more on that in a minute). Then the young brothers tell their story: they have shot air pistols and paintball guns, and now a lot of their friends are getting into shooting, and they want to do the same; it looks cool. Mr. Brookline already has his license and is, in fact, a member of the shooting range; he is just accompanying his wife to the class for support. Mrs. Brookline wants to learn how to handle their recently acquired gun. Why they have recently acquired a gun, they do not say.

Finally it is Mr. Hoodie's turn. Alone at the end of the table, hands shoved deep into his pockets, chair tilted back, he says, "I want a gun for self-defense."

He is the only person in the room who implies he might use a gun to shoot someone. I wonder if this makes him more dangerous than the rest of us, or just more honest. Jack also seems to wonder; he lingers longest with Mr. Hoodie, asking follow-up questions: Do you have a job that requires you to worry about your safety? *No.* Live in an area that feels particularly unsafe? *No.* Have you ever shot a gun before? *Yes.* What kind of gun was it? *A*

Glock. (Later my husband will say: "Of course it was.")

The ice now broken, Jack wraps up: "People own firearms for a lot of reasons." He gestures toward me. "Some people want to have fun—"

"I didn't say fun."

My tone is sharper than I intend. Jack blinks, and I'm a little embarrassed. For some reason it feels important to let this group of people I will never see again know that I do not derive pleasure from shooting things.

"It's just that I would never use the word *fun* in this context."

Jack gives me a look. "Let's move on."

⁓

My husband got his first pistol permit (Firearms Identification Card) at sixteen when some friends were going down to the cop shop to apply for theirs and suggested he roll along. He remembers the process as pretty seamless: Four teenage boys stride into the Fitchburg, Massachusetts, police department and request permission to legally shoot things. The chief looks them over briefly and hands out the permits. My husband, I should remind you, is White.

His first gun came a few years later, a housewarming gift from his father for his new bachelor pad. It was an M1 carbine left over, his father said, from the war. That gun was eventually stolen during a break-in, but years later my husand got another one. His work buddies often went to the range after a long day of engineering, and he sometimes tagged along. The first few times he borrowed a friend's gun, but he knew that generosity would not last: "It's like a car—people will let you use theirs once or twice, but after that, you'd better get your own."

A perfect analogy, I tell him. Americans are very intimate with, and very possessive of, their cars.

It turns out he had this gun when we met, though I did not know it. When we got serious, when it became clear we would be sharing a home and a life, my husband sold the firearm. "I knew how you felt about guns," he later told me. "I didn't want anything to stand in the way of us."

Who would have thought one of the great romantic gestures of my life would involve a man quietly getting rid of a gun?

All of which explains his surprise, years later, when I raised the possibility of bringing a firearm into our home. It was the fall of 2020. George Floyd had been murdered, the latest victim in an endless stream. The birther president was ramping up his lies. Armed White cultists roamed the country, giant flags with the name of their idol waving from the back of their trucks. They chanted maniacally at rallies. They intimidated voters. They tried to run people off the road. The cops winked and smiled.

"Are you afraid?" my husband asked. "Is that why you want to get a gun?"

"Not afraid," I said. "Pissed."

For three hours we work our way through the NRA book:

safe gun handling, safe storage, types of ammunition, shooting positions, parts of the pistol and how they work, how to clear a gun that jams.

At one point Jack asks a question about misfires, and I answer it. He looks surprised. "How did you know that?"

"It just makes sense," I say, because it does, and because even here I am the eternal good student, always wanting to give the right answer, even if the question is about guns.

Then Jack announces it is time for live fire. He takes the two brothers and Mr. Hoodie into the range first, leaving the rest of us behind to take the required written test. Jack encourages us to work together to answer the fifty questions, reminds us to check the book if we get stuck. This is a test everyone is meant to pass.

Then it's our turn to enter the range. My hands shake as I slip on my safety glasses and put in the earplugs. It strikes me that I am about to step knowingly and willingly into a room filled with armed strangers, most of them male, most of them White. This seems like insanity. I am astonished that people do this routinely, consider it fun. What is the positionality—the unearned, unexamined, unshakable social identity—that makes stepping into a room full of armed strangers feel like a way to increase one's safety instead of a way to endanger it? What is the version of history in which these facts—White men, guns, shooting—turn out well for someone like me?

Jack ushers us all into the anteroom, pausing to scoop a live round off the floor. Then he opens the door to the range. Silence.

"Looks like we have the range to ourselves today," says Jack. I nearly tremble with relief.

The area where the shooters stand is smaller than I expected, only slightly larger than the conference room we just left. Eight or ten stalls, each the size of a shower, are separated only by what looks to me like a slightly upgraded office-cubicle barrier. Jack steps into the first one, reminds us of the three safety rules, hands us empty magazines and bullets to load in them, and then unpacks his gun. It's a .22. He dismantles it with a few swift movements, showing us the parts: action, barrel, stock. I have never seen a gun this close, but even my decidedly non-mechanical brain can understand how it works. Such a simple, simple machine.

"Who wants to go first?"

I shake my head. My husband steps up, unloads his first clip at a rapid pace. Jack pulls in the target, compliments my husband on his aim, and advises him to slow down. My husband breathes, takes his time emptying the next three magazines. I watch his face. When Jack hands him the peppered target, he smiles.

"Your turn." Jack looks at me.

"I'm nervous."

"Don't be," he says. "I'll take care of you."

It's a nice reassurance, but I marvel at his certainty. A person he has known less than four hours stands six inches away, holding a loaded gun. I could drop the weapon, or jerk uncontrollably, or turn it on him before he had a chance to react. Anything could happen; anything always can. All safety is an illusion, but maybe it doesn't feel that way if your position in society has not only given you power but also protected you from the experience of being, and of feeling, powerless.

Taking a deep breath, I pick up the gun. It is neither light nor heavy, just a thing, an object, cool to the touch. As directed, I keep it pointed in a safe direction, downrange toward the paper target twenty feet from where I stand. I pull the trigger, bracing for recoil, but there is none, really. I finish the three magazines as quickly as possible, put the gun down. My husband beams, proud of me, but I avoid his eyes.

Jack holds up my target. "I bet you're the kind of person who is good at everything."

This is flattery, the kind of thing a good salesman says to a potential client. But I feel too grubby for flattery, too ashamed for false modesty. "Actually, I am," I say bluntly. I do not say that this is one of the things that frightens me.

❧

Why do you want a gun? My friend is appalled at what I have just told her, shocked at my change of heart. I explain as best I can, trying not to sound sheepish. My friend is skeptical. My friend is White. My Black friends, when I tell them, ask where the class was given and how much it cost. My family—among them a police officer, many veterans, and several longtime legal gun owners—offers practical advice: size, cost, caliber.

Why do you want a gun?

A gun-owning friend, helping me fill out the required paperwork, says the right response to this question is "For all legal purposes." He is a Black man, and the irony of the statement does not escape him. Rarely has the law been a Black person's friend.

Why do you want a gun?

"It's a skill," says my husband. Like riding a motorcycle or changing a tire or starting a campfire. That there is skill involved in accurately propelling a small metal object long distances into a designated spot, I cannot argue. Nor can I argue that people should not take pleasure in possessing such a skill. I only wonder what all that practicing is in preparation for. What, exactly, are you practicing to hit?

"Others own pistols for personal protection," the NRA guide says.

My husband thinks this is the reason I am suddenly interested in firearms. He knows the long, bloody history of White supremacy in this country, sees the emboldened anger, the rising violence. Even before the 2016 election we'd fantasized about moving abroad after retirement, finally leaving it all behind. Retirement is coming, but in the meantime we still live here. In the meantime we see what is clearly to be seen.

He says that even after I learn to shoot and safely handle our firearm, I will need regular visits to the shooting range to keep up my skills. I disagree. Say I do not need to become a markswoman. Tell him I only want to learn how to safely load, unload, and carry a weapon, how to store it properly so that no unauthorized users can find or wield it, how to keep from shooting myself in the foot.

"Survival is not my goal," I tell him gently.

If a civil war breaks out, I say, if violent White mobs begin roaming the country as they have done in the past, I will not worry about precision shooting. I intend to sit on my porch with my legally acquired handgun and as much ammunition as I have and perhaps a bottle of Scotch and take them as they come. I say as much to my husband. My husband, understandably, is shocked. He's not sure he believes me. I'm pretty sure he should.

"Are you afraid?" my husband asks.

Only of my anger. Only of becoming like them.

Is it possible to be angry without being violent? Is it possible to live in a violent society without becoming that way?

They march in Charlottesville, Virginia, chanting about replacement. They run down Heather Heyer like a dog. I sit at home and watch, angry.

They march through Washington, DC, shouting, "Reclaim America!" escorted by police. I sit at home, law-abiding, an exemplary citizen. Furious.

In Texas they try to run a Biden campaign bus off the road. In Oregon a Republican legislator lets them saunter armed into the state capitol. They try to kidnap the governor of Michigan.

They storm the United States Capitol, smashing windows, assaulting cops, chasing a Black officer up the stairs like a lynch mob running through the Mississippi woods, slinging racial epithets. They invade our government while waving the flag of slavery. "This is our house!" they chant.

At home I watch the television, fists balled. Our house? Our house? This house that sits on a bloody foundation, which rests on stolen land? This house painted on the outside but inside left to crumble and rot? This house that has room for all but also locked doors and hidden keys? This house?

This house is not your house. This house is either everyone's house or it is no one's.

That's what I want to defend.

Traveling Is Not a Luxury

Part I: Why I Travel

My matriarchal lineage is rich with itchy-footed women, women ready and willing, if not always eager, to get up and go. My great, great, great grandmother traveled from Georgia to Missisisspi; the circumstances are murky but given the time period, post Civil War, I can take a guess at the reasons.

My grandmother left her home in Olive Branch, Mississippi, for nearby Memphis in search of a better life, leaving a daughter behind. That daughter, my mother, left Memphis for college and returned, then for Connecticut and returned, then for Maryland and returned, until finally, having built up the necessary momentum, she broke the gravitational pull of heartbreak and poverty and home and escaped permanently to California: Eureka, I am home. Other women in my family have traveled to Missouri and Chicago and Georgia and Nevada and Alaska and Korea and Germany. (Between just my three sisters and myself we've set foot on five of the seven continents.) Some of us traveled alone, some with others; some set out on their own volition and some were sent. Some were leaving and some were going, which is different. Some returned and some did not. A journey of a thousand miles begins with a single step, but every goodbye ain't gone.

When I was twelve my mother put the five of us children into a car and drove, with her brother, from Memphis to Sacramento in her first attempt at breaking away to the Promised Land. Memphis to Sacramento is a distance of some 2,000 miles across the North American continent: across the Mighty Mississippi and in to Arkansas; across the panhandle of Oklahoma, then a relatively quick cut through the relatively thin part of Texas; past the ancient pueblos of New Mexico and the deserts and ponderosa pines of Arizona before crossing the California line east of Barstow. I have a memory of my mother, not generally a happy woman, pulling the car to the side of the road once we'd crossed through the border checkpoint (checking then for unallowed fruit or produce, not unallowed human beings) and getting out to dance. This memory may or may not be true; either way, it speaks to how the transformational possibilities of travel were sewn into me during that journey. The landscape in California was astonishing, all strange, stucco houses and tile roofs and blazing heat without humidity, all palm trees and riotous red flowers and orange trees and, surrounding everything, the California light. The light in California is not the light in Memphis or the light in Boston or the light I have seen anywhere else in the world. The light in California is part of the reason California, despite earthquakes and droughts and taxes and houses which cost more than any house should, will never be "over," at least not until everything is over. At which point, what difference will it make?

The light and the landscape in California were amazing, but it was the change in my mother's internal landscape which astonished most. In Memphis, my mother was defeated and overwhelmed, unable to break from her depression enough to go to the grocery store. In California she got her teeth fixed and went on job interviews. Put another way: in California, she looked to the future, while in Memphis she was stuck in the present, and the present was like quicksand, dragging her down. It dragged her back to Memphis after only six months. The next few years were hard.

But travel is like education; once you have it, no one can take it away. *How are you going to keep them down on the farm now that they've seen Cal-if-for-ni-a?* For eight years after returning to Memphis my mother struggled much as before. One day, while I was away at college, I called home to find the phone disconnected. My mother had packed up and gone back to California, this time for good.

Where am I going with this? What's the thesis line here? Travel is the action of making a journey, especially to distant or foreign lands. The act of going from place to place across long distances. At fifteen I traveled alone for the first time, taking a plane from Memphis to Boston and then a chartered bus to New Hampshire for boarding school. Of the trip itself I remember little: not what the plane looked like, what meal was served (for this was back when airlines still fed you), what Logan Airport looked like during that first encounter, how I managed to find my luggage and find my trunk and find my way to the bus outside. I do remember both the gnawing fear and jumpy excitement of leaving home to live among people I did not know in a place I had never seen. And I remember, or I *think I* remember, the aching loneliness which announced itself that day and has stayed with me all my life. Announced itself, not arrived; I'd grown up in a house stuffed with siblings, had never had a bed, let alone a room or any time to myself, and yet some deep, small part of me had always been lonely. At least now, traveling, it made sense.

◆

At eighteen I took that bus from my last summer at home in Memphis to college in North Carolina. I had never seen this new place before either but by now I was accustomed to launching myself into unknown places, places full of White people. Traveling alone made me feel fearless (I wasn't) and competent (yes) and resilient (yes; anyone trapped on a Greyhound bus for twenty hours had damn well better be.) The gifts of traveling.

At twenty I boarded a plane and flew across the dark Atlantic, the first person in my immediate family to leave the US, though not the last. Intent on studying abroad but lacking a second language and too cowardly to immerse myself where

English was not dominant, I chose a semester at the University of Edinburgh. I knew zilch about Scotland or the UK in general; it didn't even occur to me that my last name was Scottish until a conductor on the train from London laughingly pointed it out. Edinburgh turned out to be beautiful and snowy and cold and old and strange, a city far more insulated and less multicultural than it is today. I found myself once again the only ink on the page, the only onyx in the snow (not "fly in the buttermilk, I hate that phrase), the only American exchange student at the university who was not White. If there were African students I never found them, or they me. On campus I hung mostly with Americans, was seen as American, was treated as such. For the first time in my life, my otherness was national not racial; this was a revelation. At the same time, away from the campus, out in the streets and alleyways of Edinburgh, I was Black first, at least until I opened my mouth. Then I was a revelation, a curiosity, yes, but a joyful one. I was treated well in shops, couldn't buy a pint in a pub. Aside from being expected to sing (which I couldn't) I had no complaints about my reception. For the first time I understood myself as both Black and American, and understood too that identity is not only multifaceted but mutable, shifting over time and over place. The gifts of travel.

Where am I going with this? What's the thesis line here? Audre Lorde wrote, "The quality of light by which we scrutinize our lives has direct bearing upon the product which we live, and upon the changes we hope to bring about through those lives."

Lorde is writing about poetry, and the ways in which poetry can serve as a gateway into the hidden inner rooms of women's lives. Hidden because western patriarchal thought taught us those rooms—our feelings, our emotions—were weak and trivial at best, hysterical and meaningless at worst. These are the rooms of ourselves about which we know the least and therefore fear the most, and that fear and removal keeps women from translating those feelings first into thought, then into language and finally into action in service of improving their lives. For this reason, Lorde writes, poetry is not a luxury for women. (Though one might reasonably argue that no one needs access into those unknown and frightening inner selves more than men.)

Travel can serve this same purpose, though through different means and in a different way. "Most people live in almost total darkness," wrote James Baldwin, but here's the thing: they don't mind it in there. It's comfortable and comforting. They can sit there in the dimness carrying on the monologue of self that passes for conversation with most people, secure in the belief that what they see is all there is. Travel, like poetry (not to mention the work of James Baldwin) raises the blinds and cleans the window. Maybe even opens the door so you can step outside.

Once I took a Greyhound bus from Memphis to Durham, a distance of nearly 800 miles which seemed much longer, like crossing the Rockies instead of the Smokies. The route went, like all travel routes in the South, through Atlanta; I transferred three times, wandered aimlessly around seedy bus stations while waiting for transfers, sat next to a man eating catfish from a greasy paper bag. Not fresh catfish. It was a miserable trip. I remember it fondly.

Once in Paris I was separated from my children on the Metro and ran frantically through the streets to the next stop trying to catch them, only to find the station closed because of a bomb scare. Once I took a six-month-old baby on a plane to Germany. Once, on a train in Italy when I was too young to respond, a man molested me in the passageway, grabbing me and sticking his tongue into my mouth before I knew what was happening. Once in Monrovia a taxi driver, driving recklessly, knocked a man from his bike and a fight ensued. I once slept in a phone booth in Zurich, at a bus station in Phoenix, at a resort hotel in Namibia that was perfectly nice except for the fact that my tour guide, who disliked me because I was wore a "SWAPO must win" pin a man I'd met in Windhoek had given me, gleefully informed me that until quite recently Black people had not been allowed to swim in the pool.

I am making it sound as if all travel involves some measure of misery. The word travel comes, as far as anyone can tell, from the Old French word *travail*, meaning to exert oneself, to labor or toil. This makes sense given the slowness, arduousness and danger of travel during ancient times. London to Canterbury is fewer than sixty miles but it took a whole lot of talking and tale-telling to get the pilgrims there and back. The road to Jherico was not for the faint of heart.

Travel need not be miserable but people who travel, first and foremost, seeking ease and amusement miss the point. (I might say this is the reason I despise Disneyland but that wouldn't be true: there are many, many reasons.) Travel is disruption, or should be. Travel, done right, means stepping outside of one's comfort zone, and nobody likes that. On that plane to Scotland as a young woman I wondered what the hell I had gotten myself into; those first weeks in Edinburgh, staring out of my dorm room at the lion-like form of Authur's Seat while the radio played a BBC jingle (*England, Scotland, Ireland, Wales!*) were some of the loneliest of my life. To survive, I had to first go deep (believing I could do this, even though no one in my family had) and then open, forcing myself beyond the comforts and restraints of the familiar and the known. (Yes, I ate haggis. Yes, it was terrible but no more so than chitterlings.) Travel, done right, is abrasive. It chafes, rubbing away the calcified outer shell of self so that something more vital can expand. Travel, done right, makes tangible and real the oft and easily avoided truth that *my* way is not *the* way but just another way among many. Travel, done right, forces you inward, like poetry, while also forcing you outward, like education. Education done right.

This is why travel, like education and home ownership, is good for people at the top of the social ladder, but critical for those on lower rungs. There's the rub, of course: travel, unlike poetry, costs money, even if it's just the cost of a bus ticket to a nearby town or the gas used as your mother drives you over to see where the White folks live. Traveling costs money and thus is often inaccessible to poor people, but, like fresh produce and a college education and quality medical care, it shouldn't be. Traveling is not a luxury for those at the bottom of the social ladder for the reason that those are the people who most need the awakening that travel can bring.

I use the word "awakening" deliberately here. One of the most cynical and successful ploys (and that's saying a lot) of rightwing ideologues in the US has been the corruption of the term "wokeness." Growing up as a child in Memphis in the 1970s, I remember folks cautioning us to "stay woke." The phrase goes back among Black people at least as far as 1923, when Marcus Garvey called people of African descent throughout the diaspora to a global consciousness: "Wake up Ethiopia! Wake up Africa!" Later the phrase "stay woke" was uttered by the great bluesman Lead Belly (Huddie Ledbetter) at the end of a protest song about the Scottsboro Boys. Lead Belly advised Black folks to be careful when traveling through the violent White supremacist and terroristic South: "So I advise everybody, be a little careful when they go along through there— best stay woke, keep their eyes open." In other words, don't sleep on America, Black people. Because America will take you out.

This is the history and origin of "wokeness," which the ideologues know full well. Now, more than ever, Black people and other people at the bottom of the American hegemony need to stay woke. Travel can help with that.

Besides, you never know when you might have to get out for good. Might have to run for your life.

Part II: Travels with the Unicorn

We land in Lisbon some twenty hours after leaving home. Neither one of us has slept: the plane was disappointingly small and predictably crowded, delayed again and again and again. Not the smoothest trip eastward across the Atlantic, but, I tell my husband, given the one my ancestors took, I cannot complain.

The woman at the rental car counter is politely condescending, warns the only cars they have are manuals, expresses surprise that we can drive standard, answers our questions about tolls as though speaking to toddlers. People always treat tourists as if they are stupid, as if unfamiliarity means an automatic lack of intelligence, as if traveling beyond one's zone of comfort means you lacked the good sense to stay home. I'm as guilty as anyone—the clumps of tourists clogging the Public Gardens near my office often put me, unfairly, in mind of cows—which is why this kind of dismissal tends to roll right off both my husband and me. We get the car.

Because I have been braving the streets of Boston for twenty years, I take first crack behind the wheel. My husband supports this joint decision; his masculinity does not melt in the passenger seat. (He will, however, insist upon driving before we leave the city.) The first few miles are anxiety-producing—unknown car, unknown city, street signs in a language we cannot understand—but then we hit a giant roundabout (there are many, many roundabouts in Portugal), cars whizzing everywhere and my husband, calmly navigating from his iPhone, says, "Third exit" and I slice the little gray Citron around the circle like I am Lewis Hamilton.

After that, the driving is easy. People in Portugal drive as though they possess both common and communal sense; in other words, not like Americans. Traffic is fast but rule-abiding: no cellphone staring, no tailgating and the passing lane is actually the passing lane. In fifteen minutes we've reached the Bairro Alto district. The streets are narrow and sometimes cobblestone, the buildings old and historic, tourists meander everywhere, stepping in front of you without a care. It feels like home. My husband spots a sign for a nearby parking garage and we make our way down a narrow, winding entrance to the dark, low-ceilinged cavern. When I pull the brake and kill the engine, we kiss and dap.

"Great job," he says.

"Go team," I say.

⌒

For the first part of my life, I traveled mostly by myself. Some of this was work-related, one huge benefit of being a journalist. I went (was sent) to Chicago, to Kentucky and Cleveland, to Salt Lake City and to Los Angeles during the riots after the beating of Rodney King. I went (was sent) to Montreal to interview the head of McGill University, to Liberia to cover the civil war and to South

Africa to fill in briefly for a colleague returning from a three-year stint. On my own I visited Montana and Arizona and New Orleans and South Carolina and Namibia, a country of astonishing beauty, wandering the capital of Windhoek for a week before joining a group tour (the wandering was great, the group tour a mistake, but that was also a learning experience: never do group tours.)

Traveling alone has its benefits. You go where you want and do what you want for as long as you so desire. Silence is easily found if you want it; if not, there are usually other people around, for better or worse. Traveling alone means no obligations, no compromises, no unwanted expenditures of energy. No resentments, except the usual resentments of travel. Traveling alone means autonomy, to the extent any human being can be truly autonomous.

Traveling alone is a perfectly fine way to travel but so is traveling as a pair, if the partnership is strong. Traveling with a partner means compromises and trade-offs, negotiations and middle grounds. It also means someone to share the driving and the map-reading and to take your hand along unknown streets.

As luck would have it, my husband and I mostly share traveling sensibilities. Each of us would rather lick the handrails in the Paris Metro than take a cruise or spend a week at a Carribean resort. We are not makers of itineraries or must-see lists, preferring to show up in a city or country and largely play things by ear. We like to keep things moving, rarely spending more than three or four nights in a single place; if we like it, we can always come back and in the meantime, there are usually interesting places to explore nearby. We're satisfied scanning the outside of certain places—the Tower of London, the Colosseum in Rome—and have zero interest in standing in long lines to see more. We dislike amusement parks and have seen enough cathedrals, preferring to wander off the beaten path. We take hiccups like steady rain in Quebec City or the total absence of taxis at the ferry in Malta at 2 am as part of the adventure. We don't subscribe to the notion that the farther one travels the longer one must stay to make it worthwhile, sometimes leaving the country for less than a week. We once flew to Rennes, France, for the weekend to see my son who was spending his junior high school year abroad. Rennes is a lovely old French city but, really, two days was plenty for us.

While my husband and I share traveling sensibilities, in other ways we differ, and these ways are interesting. For one thing, I do not travel abroad expecting to be welcome in foreign places, don't leave home assuming people will be happy to see me. I like to travel incognito, not drawing attention to myself, because my blood memory tells me that attention=trouble. To be fair, this has almost exclusively been true in the States, where the sudden, unsolicited attention of White people should always be treated as a potential threat to one's life. Abroad, stares and whispering usually just mean curiosity, which is tiring but fine. Traveling away from home, my reflexive hope is for indifference at worst, benign tolerance at best; anything above that I take as a lovely and pleasant surprise.

Until we began traveling together, it never occurred to my husband, who as I have mentioned is White, that there might be places in the world where he might be seen not just as foreign but as undesirable. In Eastern Europe or South America or the southern United States, he traveled lightly, expecting, if not outright welcome, certainly not animosity. The only issue along these lines he ever encountered was being called "round eyes" by some children in China, which amused him. My son spent a summer in China during college. He heard and experienced a lot worse, and not from kids. And I have taught many wonderful Chinese students who confessed—sheepishly, apologetically—that their parents had warned them passionately about the dangers of Black people. My husband would happily venture back to China, a vast and complex and beautiful country, but I'm not really interested.

Am I treated differently traveling alone than when we travel together? Honestly, it's hard to say. By the time my husband and I met I had crossed the threshold of fifty, had passed through sufficient elite institutions and met enough wealthy people to no longer be impressed, was old enough and smart enough and bored enough to walk into any place, no matter how fancy or wealthy or White, like I belonged there, like I owned it. As in life, this goes a long, long way in travel. Most people treat you like they sense you expect to be treated. They take their cues from you.

But there are times when I'd rather not be bothered, and during those times being bothered is easier for him. Driving past the Trump flags and/or Confederate flags in central New Hampshire or western Massachusetts or coastal North Carolina or rural California or other parts of the country that might as well be Mississippi with better scenery, I'm content to stay in the car when my husband goes into the gas station or convenience store or coffee shop. I don't actually expect to encounter people wearing hoods or plotting treasonous rebellion against the United States. But if such people were encountered, my husband could pass undetected. Whiteness as invisibility cloak.

But there are other differences in how we travel. One time, in Quito, Ecuador, my husband arranged for someone to pick us up at the airport and drive us to our hotel. This is something I would never have done, would never have even considered doing. For one thing, the poor child inside still defaults to finding the cheapest mode of transportation, while the city-dweller prides herself on learning how to navigate public transit. In Paris this tendency resulted in my sister, kids and myself dragging our heavy bags nearly a mile from the subway to our rented flat (to be fair, they were mostly my sister's heavy bags, since I never pack more than I can comfortably carry.)

In Quito, my husband also arranged for a lovely man named Xaviar to give us a tour of the city and surrounding areas, including a ride on the TelefériQo up the flanks of Volcán Pichincha to the top of Cruz Loma for a spectacular view. Before meeting me, my husband had traveled abroad mostly for business and this is how businessmen travel, having the way paved before them. Though we were, of course, polite, respectful and generous to Xaviar, having someone chauffeur me through a foreign city made me feel like a privileged American tourist, tossing my weight and money around. Still, I have to admit to understanding the appeal. We saw far more of the city than we would have on our own, learned about the history and current political situation and stopped for lunch at a spot that would have been invisible to us otherwise. When a terrible mudslide hit Quito a few weeks after we returned home, my husband reached out to Xaviar on WhatsApp to check on him and his family. Thankfully everyone was fine.

In Quarteria, Portugal, the beach is overshadowed by tall, ugly apartment buildings and packed so tightly with people there is little room to spread a towel. We get in the car and meander the highway, ending up in a town called Loulé where the locals ignore us as we walk past old men drinking coffee and arguing politics at a cafe, stumble into a courtyard where an orchestra is rehearsing for a concert, have a drink on the patio of a lively bar. For dinner we find a small restaurant whose owner seats us at one of two tables in the alley outside the front door, telling us to ignore the car driving straight toward us. It's his father, coming to drop something off.

In Memphis we peek over the fence at Graceland, but neither one of us wants to go in. For one thing, the entrance fee is more than seventy dollars, which is straight-up, laughably ridiculous. For another thing, no offense but: Elvis? My husband asks me again about being in Memphis the day the King died and driving with my mother past Graceland and watching the White people wail and faint and moan. I tell him, lowering my voice to be sensitive, though all the people peeking over the fence are Black (all the people taking the tour buses up to the house are White) that we were shocked; as far as we knew White people had very little reason to cry about public events and rarely did, unlike my mother. My husband laughs delightedly.

We drive around visiting the stations of my childhood: our little brick house, our little brick elementary school, the church of my youth. We visit my aunt, one of the few relatives still living in Memphis, though she doesn't really live in Memphis but in a suburb called, I kid you not, White Haven. Because you have to, we walk down Beale Street, a real, if downtrodden street during my childhood, now a cheap version of Bourbon Street. We visit the Civil Rights Museum, then, to shake off the clouds of history, walk the park that lines the Mighty Mississippi until we find a place where we can lean off a muddy hillside and dip in our hands. This is a ritual; everywhere we travel we touch the water if we can. We've touched the Pacific in California, the Atlantic in Maine and North Carolina and Portugal, the St. Lawrence in Quebec. In Chicago, Lake Michigan.

On our last day in Memphis we visit the Stax Museum, an unexpected delight. After wandering the exhibits for an hour we find ourselves on a dance floor. A disco ball spins above , sending sparkles of light across the walls. The "Theme From *Shaft*" booms from the speakers.

Naturally we dance.

Run for Your Life

In the years after my divorce I underwent a prolonged emotional crisis involving bouts of depression, mass consumption of French fries and a stubborn habit of falling in love with men who did not love me in return. For the most part these men were not bad people, were, as they hacked their way through the swamp of midlife dating, not deliberately destructive, or at least no more so than I. There was, however, one person whose bad behavior was intentional, who was, in his dealings with women in general and me in particular, selfishly, gleefully, actively unkind. This person reveled in the notion of having an upper hand in relationships, of power as aphrodisiac. Alternately attentive and dismissive, lying and truthful, nastily disparaging and lavish with praise, he kept me off-center and I allowed it, drawn to the treatment like a cat toward catnip. Catnip sprinkled on coals. It was a messy, painful, damaging connection, not good for anyone.

My friends, watching from the sidelines, frequently registered their concern and disapproval, but I remained unhearing and unmoved. Eventually one said, "You know, this is an abusive relationship."

I bristled. An abusive relationship? The summation rankled. The man in question had never hit me, never become physical, never so much as threatened violence. Yes, he was a jerk, a selfish user without remorse. But an abuser? Wouldn't that make me a victim? Wouldn't that make me weak?

The definition of abuse is *to use wrongly or improperly, use to bad effect or for a bad purpose, to misuse; to hurt or injure by maltreatment; to treat a person or animal with cruelty or violence.* Not all of these things were true about the relationship, but a few of them were. Enough to fail to ease my discomfort. Enough to make me think. If the situation was not precisely abusive, it was certainly dysfunctional, and the primary distinction, I came to realize, was the issue of power. In my case, the only power this guy had over me was the power I handed to him.

In the summer of 2020, after a police officer in Wisconsin shot Jacob Blake in the back seven times as he leaned into the car where his children sat, I came across a video clip on the internet. It wasn't the shooting; I have not watched a video of police shooting or ramming or kneeling on the necks of Black people since Rodney King. The clip I stumbled across was an interview with basketball coach Doc Rivers. He sat on a bench after some game, discussing not fouls and shots but the police shooting of Mr. Blake and other Black people, the cynical fear mongering of then-President Donald Trump and other Republicans, the way peaceful Black protest is met with force while violent White protest is met with smiles.

Forcing back tears, Doc said: "It's amazing why we keep loving this country and this country doesn't love us back."

Well, there you go, I thought. *That* is an abusive relationship.

∽

According to the National Coalition Against Domestic Violence, a person experiencing abuse may: be embarrassed or fear judgment and stigmatization; love the person who is abusing them and believe that they will change; deny that anything is wrong or excuse the other person. The person may also behave in ways that can be difficult for people outside the relationship to understand. These behaviors include: refusing to leave the relationship; believing that the other person is powerful or knows everything; when things are calm, idealizing the person who carried out the abuse; believing that they deserve the abuse.

∽

When I was a child the Fourth of July passed with little fuss. Maybe my mother burned some hot dogs on our small charcoal grill, maybe my uncle brought over some sparklers and we ran around fizzling in the dark. Even the Bicentennial in 1976, which swept up the nation in a fervor of nostalgia and self-love, meant to us mostly televised fireworks and tall ships (both disappointing) and everything in the supermarket suddenly packaged in red, White and blue. Had you asked me the reason for the celebration, I, being an excellent student, would have given the correct answer, just as I would have identified the five columns used in classical architecture. Neither the nation being celebrated nor a Doric column had I ever seen.

The first time I thought of myself as American was the first time I left America. Writing that line reminds me of the old joke about the elderly fish who swims by two younger fish. "How's the water today?" he asks. "What's water?" they reply. But this was not precisely my experience. From the day I set foot on the campus of Phillips Exeter Academy at age fifteen I understood America was the water in which I swam. I just did not think of myself as one of the fish.

As mentioned previously, during my junior year in college, I left America to spend a semester at the University of Edinburgh. I was eager to go, eager to get away from roommates and failed crushes and campus cliques and the ever-present specter of racism and race in America. I had been told Edinburgh, like London, was a multicultural city, which turned out (at that time) to be not precisely the case. The people I met in class and in the dorms and in the pubs and in the shops were Scottish, English, Welsh, French, Spanish, Italian, American and almost exclusively White. I stood out.

"Where are you from?" people asked over and over, not hostile but gaping, puzzled, perplexed.

"Memphis."

"Ah," they responded. "American." As if that explained everything.

Baldwin wrote, "I love America more than any other country in the world, and, exactly for this reason, I insist on the right to criticize her perpetually." But, of course, quotes out of context are dangerous. ("When one begins to live by habit and quotation one has begun to stop living.") Baldwin's words about loving America come from *Notes of a Native Son*, his first nonfiction collection of essays, published in 1955 when he was barely thirty-one. Before the murders of Medgar, Martin and Malcolm. Before the nation turned its back on even the modest gains of the Civil Rights Movement. Before the White backlash which resulted in the election of Ronald Reagan and the White backlash which resulted in the election of Donald Trump.

I wonder what Baldwin would say now?

Did I ever love America? I'm trying to remember. Walking the cobblestone sidewalks of Edinburgh in the late 1980s I sometimes felt homesick, but the home for which I yearned were the people who loved me, my family and friends. I missed being around Black people, missed church and Saturday night card-playing and black-eyed peas on New Year's Day. I did not miss the nation's b-movie president or his folksy dog-whistling. Did not miss the worship of wealth or the convenient demonization of the impoverished. Did not miss all the efforts to keep the dreamer dreaming, the obsessive consuming and the insipid television shows and the outsized attention to professional sports. I did not miss the cars or the flag-waving or the neverending cereal aisles. Did I miss America? What is America? The people? The idea? The land? I love the light in California, the levees that rise above the Mississippi River in my hometown, the leaves of New England in fall. I also love the tiled sidewalks of Lisbon, the White sand beaches of Monrovia, the apricot dunes of Namibia. I love cornbread and gumbo and apple pie, but also harissa. I love Black people from these United States—Afro/African/Black Americans—and all that we have created. I love *Soul Train* and Marvin Gaye and Aretha Franklin and Black English and Afros and Toni Morrison and James Baldwin. There is much *from* and *of* America that I love deeply, even desperately. But do I love America?

There's a video of Baldwin I've watched a dozen times. He is being interviewed by Dr. Kenneth Clark on the day of the infamous meeting between Robert F. Kennedy and a group of Black writers, actors and activists. Baldwin says:

"A boy last week, he was sixteen, in San Francisco told me—on television, thank God we got him to talk, maybe somebody will start to listen—he said, 'I've got no country, I've got no flag.' And I couldn't say, 'You do.' I don't have any evidence to prove that he does."

Baldwin spoke those lines in 1963. One hundred and sixteen years earlier Frederick Douglas said:

I cannot agree with my friend Mr. Garrison, in relation to my love and attachment to this land. I have no love for America, as such; I have no patriotism. I have no country. What country have I? The institutions of this country do not know me, do not recognize me as a man. I am not thought of, spoken of, in any direction, out of the anti-slavery ranks, as a man. I am not thought of, or spoken of, except as a piece of property . . . Now, in such a country as this, I cannot have patriotism. The only thing that links me to this land is my family, and the painful consciousness that here and there are three millions of my fellow-creatures, groaning beneath the iron rod of the worst despotism that could be devised . . .

When my son came to me at sixteen and said he wanted to spend his junior year of high school in France I said yes without hesitation. When acquaintances (most of them White) asked if I wasn't afraid to let him go I pointed out that my son was a young Black man growing up in America: I was afraid to let him step out of the house. Though of course I worried about him being so far away, part of me slept easier at night with him out of the jurisdiction of the American police. More importantly, I wanted him to have the experience of living somewhere other than the United States so that he would know, deep down in his cells, that he could, and that it would be fine, perhaps even better. I encouraged my daughter to take a semester abroad in college and when she did I was very, very glad. I wanted my children to be able to pack their bags and leave America if they needed to do so. I wanted them to be easy, confident citizens of the world.

Love America? Ask me tomorrow, or maybe later today. Hate America? That's one easy: the opposite of love is not hate, it's indifference. If Black people hated America, America would be constantly on fire—and Black people would all be dead. Instead of just some of us.

The only people I have ever heard express real and violent hatred for America are White. One semester a student—White, male, embittered by Bernie Sander's failure to win the presidential race—wrote explicitly and directly of his hatred of the nation in a paper refuting the idea that Black Americans have been and can be the perfectors of American democracy. "I want to see the whole thing burn to the ground," he wrote. Another White student was less violent but equally detesting, expressing his belief that reform was impossible, radical change never to come. He said, startling even me: "America is a disease."

My Black students express mostly disappointment and bewilderment. Why weren't they taught about David Walker and Maria Stewart and Claude McKay? Why have they never heard of Harriet Jacobs or Frances Harper or even Audre Lorde? How can the issues of state-sanctioned violence against Black people, of segregated housing and embedded poverty and segregated, second-rate education and substandard healthcare and stereotyping of Black women and the adultification of Black children—how can these issues *still* plague Black America when people were pointing them out fifty, a hundred, 150 years ago? They are crushed that the worldwide protests and corporate posturing after the murder of George Floyd produced more backlash than lasting change. They see that what they thought was a slow march of progress, plodding but straight, is really more of a carousel, going round and round again. They want to know what it will take to actually bring an end to structural White supremacy and anti-Black racism. They want to know when we will finally overcome?

≈

Right around the same time as the shooting of Jacob Blake, I came across a conversation on Twitter regarding the letter Hannah Arendt famously wrote to James Baldwin in 1962 after his essay "Letter from a Region in My Mind" appeared in *The New Yorker*. In the letter, Arendt first offers Baldwin some faint praise for his essay, calling it "a political event of a very high order, I think." She then goes on to object to Baldwin's concluding sentiment, saying that since the Negro question is a question which "concerns us all," she feels within her rights to speak:

> What frightened me in your essay was the gospel of love which you begin to preach at the end. In politics, love is a stranger, and when it intrudes upon it nothing is

being achieved except hypocrisy. All the characteristics you stress in the Negro people: their beauty, their capacity for joy, their warmth, and their humanity, are well-known characteristics of all oppressed people. They grow out of suffering and they are the proudest possession of all pariahs. Unfortunately, they have never survived the hour of liberation by even five minutes. Hatred and love belong together, and they are both destructive; you can afford them only in the private (sic) and, as a people, only so long as you are not free.

The person posting the letter on Twitter was not impressed. *"Hannah really sent this to James Baldwin"* they wrote. *"This is the kind of shit White people feel ok doing."*

That's not wrong. Arendt's letter reminds me of emails I've received over the years, emails which assert the writer's right to object, to explain, to correct. One White woman presumed to argue with me about the central motivating force behind the self-destructive anger of the protagonist of my first novel. It was not, she insisted, anger at the insidious tentacles of White supremacy but something else. Anything else.

But although I think Arendt is wrong in some ways, I cannot say she is completely incorrect. Her assertion that the beauty, warmth and *humanity* which Baldwin celebrates as part of African American culture are characteristics arising *solely* from our oppression is certainly incorrect, evidence not only of her anti-Blackness (on full display in other essays) but also her simple ignorance of African American culture and the various African cultures from which it springs. As a particular kind of social media pundit is ever-eager to point out, the peoples who became African Americans were hardly the first in the history of the world to be oppressed, exploited, enslaved, but few others have created so much out of the experience. The blues and jazz and hip hop, the sorrow songs and spirituals, the poems of Frances Harper and Langston Hughes and Rita Dove and Jericho Brown, the novels of Hurston and Ellison and Morrison, the plays of Hansberry and Parks and Wilson, the art of Lawrence and Savage and Ringgold, the food and the fashion and the hairstyles and the language ("If Black English ain't a language, then tell me what is?") all this is a mighty river, altered and shaped by its channeling through 400 years of White supremacist oppression but not there sourced. If you want to explain Black folks in America, you have to look at the headwaters.

But in the essay in question, "Down at the Cross," Baldwin seems to suggest that Black people, given power and privilege, would not behave as badly as White people have behaved:

"And one felt that if one had had the White man's worldly advantages, one would never have become as bewildered and as joyless and as thoughtlessly cruel as he."

Arendt objects to this valorization. All the characteristics of Black people that Baldwin touts—"their beauty, their capacity for joy, their warmth and their humanity"—are, she says, well-known characteristics of all oppressed people, not likely to survive the journey from bottom to top.

In this I think Arendt is probably right—though I would like to live long enough to test the theory. If Black Americans have, in general, a clearer grasp on reality than our White fellow citizens, it's only because we've needed it to survive. If we possess more warmth and beauty and capacity for joy, it's only because without these things we would not have survived this far and this long. If Black people in America are, in general, more humane than White people, it is only because we have evolved, from necessity, cultures of connection and kinship and mutuality, have built these beliefs into a Black tradition, defined by Baldwin as "a field of manners and rituals of intercourse that can sustain a man once he's left his father's house." But the strength of these traditions, their ability to withstand the American ethos of selfishness and individual gain cannot be assumed. Black people are people, too, with all the individual human capacity for greed and cruelty and spite. One might ask the Kru and Grebo peoples of West Africa how the freedom-seeking Americo-Liberian colonizers handled things. As one example.

I think Baldwin knew this. His emphasis, it seems to me, rests on the *joylessness* of White American life and the *thoughtlessness* of White American cruelty, not on the cruelty itself. Setting aside the fact that Black folks have never demanded to be on top, just to have the boots removed from our necks, Black Americans might well become as cruel as White Americans were power ever to shift so significantly—but we could never become as innocent. It is the innocence which constitutes the crime.

At bottom it seems Baldwin and Arendt are worried about opposite sides of the same coin: Arendt is worried what Black people will do to White people if we were ever to gain power. Baldwin, having seen clearly what power has done to White folks, is worried what it would do to us.

As to whether or not love *belongs* in the public realm, I have no idea. Certainly the opposite of love, which is a chilling indifference, is fully present in American public life. So, of course, is hatred. Hatred permeates the American public sphere, blossoming always, amply fed through roots of power and greed and fear. Love is not the answer to power or greed or fear, or to the hatred fed by those waters. Black people will never love White Americans into letting go of power. Black people will never love America into facing itself.

Love may well be a stranger in mainstream American politics, which is to say in the political arena of White supremacy. This is not only because Whiteness, by necessity, demonizes non-Whiteness, but also because Whiteness, by creation, had no actual need for love. The elite planters and colonial governors who—law by law, regulation by regulation—created Whiteness in Jamestown had no lost love for the poor European masses they were gifting with the legacy, only a need to divide the lower classes and thus ensure their labor supply.

The European indentured servants and other unlanded folk for whom Whiteness was created did not need self-love to go along with the game—only fear of the very real detriments of being Black. That America is a country pathologically bereft of love is self-evident. Columbine. Sandy Hook. The list goes on and on.

But love can never be a stranger to Black politics; Black protest and Black resistance extend not from fear or hatred or rage. Harriet Tubman risked her life over and over again out of love. Frederick Douglass risked his freedom on the abolition circuit, telling America the truth about itself out of love. Ida B. Wells fought lynching out of love. Ella Baker, Fannie Lou Hamer, Martin Luther King, Stokely Carmichael, the founders of the Movement for Black Lives and, yes, yes, yes, Malcolm X—these people (and so many more) acted and continue to act from one source only: love for their families, their communities, themselves. Love is the necessary basis for sustained, grassroots Black politics in these United States.

It's the only possible thing that can keep a person in the fight.

∾

The cycle of abuse is a social cycle theory explaining patterns of intimate partner violence developed in 1979 by Lenore Walker, an American psychologist and author who later inexplicably ruined her career by testifying for OJ Simpson. The term describes the cycling patterns which characterize many abusive relationships: rising tension, incident, reconciliation, calm. These periods of reconciliation and calm—and the hopes they raise for an end to the abuse—are part of the reason the abused find it difficult to "just leave" the relationship. *See,* they tell themselves, *things are not always terrible. He can be wonderful sometimes. She can be good.*

I thought about this theory a lot during the summer of 2020, as the United States of America spasmed once again through a "racial awakening." That's one of the media catchphrases, meant, as Baldwin would tell us, to obscure as much as reveal: *racial awakening. Racial unrest. Racial injustice.* Perhaps my favorite was *"the twin pandemics of COVID-19 and systemic racism."* As if a system of violent White supremacy had popped out of nowhere and spread like wildfire devoid of human intention, taking everyone by surprise.

That White Americans were shocked—shocked!—to witness the casual, state-sanctioned murder of George Floyd and the reckless, state-sanctioned murder of Breonna Taylor and the casual, state-sanctioned shooting of Jacob Blake IN FRONT OF HIS CHILDREN, shocked to discover that "law and order" really means "control and kill the Black people," surprised to discover marching neo-Nazis and gun-toting "proud" (laugh) boys in their midst, stunned to learn how many of their friends and neighbors and family members tacitly or explicitly supported all of this—none of this surprised me. *It's the innocence which constitutes the crime.*

What surprised me was the surprise of some Black people, the surprise of some of my students, some of my family, some of my friends. Not shock. No sane, thoughtful Black person in America can ever be shocked to discover that White supremacy and anti-Black racism are alive and well and living in Georgia . . . and New York and Oregon and Arizona and Maine, etc. I don't know a single Black person who actually thought racism was "over," but I do know a few who said something like this to me:

"I knew it was still real but I guess I didn't think it was *this* bad. I didn't realize how much they hated us."

Really? I ask, banging my head. Why not?

Obama, of course. Beyonce and Chadwick and Kendrick Lamar. Oprah! Sure, they knew Mississippi was garbage, but the country wasn't Mississippi, or Florida or Arizona or Missouri or New Hampshire or Maine. Yes, they took great pains to teach their sons and daughters to be oh-so-careful around cops but that was just life, wasn't it? Yes, they had to take down all their family photos and Black art when selling their house but the appraisal was fine after they did that and the house sold. Yes, all those White folks were promoted over them despite knowing squat about the work, but their boss always sent a lovely card at Christmas. Yes, yes, yes, but.

Periods of reconciliation and calm. Everybody gets off on Martin Luther King Jr. Day. Here's Juneteenth as a national holiday. The cycle of abuse.

Had he lived, were Death not the ruthless, thieving asshole

he is, leaving too long the evil, snatching far too soon the good, James Balwin would have turned 100 in 2024. That puts him right in between my grandmother, who was born in 1919, lived a hard life shaped by poverty and racism, and died too young, and my mother, who is battered and bruised but still standing. I am thinking of generations.

I was born in 1964, which makes me either the tail end of the Baby Boomers or the unacknowledged start of Generation X, i.e. the Lost Generation, part 2, i.e. the Sandwich Generation, i.e. the Baby Bust. My children and my students are the iGeneration, Generation Z. (Why did we start so late in the alphabet, naming ourselves? Did we expect to run out of humanity?)

I am thinking of generations.

Baldwin in his famous, riveting debate at the University of Cambridge against the unctuous William F Buckley:

In the case of the American Negro, from the moment you are born every stick and stone, every face, is White. Since you have not yet seen a mirror, you suppose you are, too. It comes as a great shock around the age of 5, 6, or 7 to discover that the flag to which you have pledged allegiance, along with everybody else, has not pledged allegiance to you. It comes as a great shock to see Gary Cooper killing off the Indians, and although you are rooting for Gary Cooper, that the Indians are you.

I am thinking of generations: "five or six or seven."

The students at the college where I teach are traumatized by the racism of their professors and fellow students. Done violence by being asked to watch *Birth of a Nation* in a film studies class (with warnings and context.) Damaged when the campus newspaper highlights Black Lives Matter by writing about a White student whose father has cut her off for supporting the movement. Traumatized by racist Zoom bombings and White students who practice racism aloud for the hell of it. They demand not only change but apologies. They believe apologies will help. I don't know.

I am thinking of generations.

Some of us came of age expecting to be hated and some of us came of age expecting to be accepted grudgingly and resentfully and some of us came of age expecting to be loved. My heart breaks for my students; expecting to be loved makes everything worse.

But Doc Rivers is three years older than I am. He should damn well know better.

❧

Research has documented how much domestic abusers across cultures and geography tend to follow the same script. Techniques such as isolation, alternating punishment and reward, projecting omnipotence while cultivating anxiety and despair—these are the universal language of oppression, traversing the globe. These techniques directly mirror those in the "Chart of Coercion" created by social scientist Albert Biderman to explain not domestic abuse but the behavior of captured American soldiers who cooperated with their North Korean captors during the Korean War.

But while the techniques may be the same, researchers suggest there is more than one *type* of abuser. Elizabeth Gilchrist of the University of Edinburgh found that the research generally divides abusers into two broad groups: an antisocial group who abuse instrumentally (which is to say with calculation), and an emotionally-volatile group who abuse out of negative emotion and impulsivity. "While the above typology research has not expanded into a specific exploration of the cognitions underlying abusiveness," she writes, "the general attitudes displayed appear to indicate cognitions themed by *hostility, selfishness, entitlement* and *narcissism* in the generally violent/antisocial abuser and *fear, dependence, anger, external blaming* and *jealousy* in the emotionally volatile group."

Using this taxonomy, America might reasonably be diagnosed, in its relationship to Black people, as both antisocial *and* emotionally volatile. But if pushed to choose a diagnosis (for, say, example, a court case or a medical claim), I'd have to go with—and this is a tough one, an exceedingly close call and I am willing to be challenged—emotionally volatile.

Fear. Dependence. Anger. External blaming. Jealousy.

Check, check, check, check and check.

This is my professional opinion.

～

We should have known it would come to this. If we're being honest, we have to admit that things were far from sweetness and light even at the beginning. All the abduction and buying and enslavement, all the whippings and raping, the branding of skin and wrenching of children from our arms. Not exactly days of wine and roses. You told us all the violence and exploitation was for our own good, that we were lazy (hah!) and childlike and helpless without you, that you knew what was best and that God approved. We disagreed with that, but you had the dogs and the guns and the armed patrols, so we pretended to go along, resisting in whatever ways we could that did not get us killed. Or sometimes did. When that first, terrible part finally ended—our honeymoon!—we had high hopes that things would get better, that you would change. People like Booker T. Washington told us that you would. All we had to do was stay in our place, not ask too much and smile. Always smile.

Well. We suspected this was all so much bullshit. But what choice did we have? We put lye on our hair and bleach on our skin to look more like you. We made fun of ourselves for your amusement, shuffling and bucking our eyes. We wrote poems and stories and plays, painted paintings and crafted sculptures, danced like no one has ever danced before and, of course, made music, world-changing music. All for ourselves but also as proof, as if proof were needed or would be heard. We let you take (again) what you wanted, which was everything: political power, economic dominance, a delusional belief in your own superiority. The land. When we were feeling strong or angry or fed up and tried (again) to resist we usually got beaten so badly we were unable to continue fighting. Or else we just died. When the abuse got really bad, when you were raging around the house, drunk with power and soul-sick with guilt and fear, bashing us with your fists, we tried to leave you, tried slipping away to northern cities and northern towns. Turned out you were there too, wearing different uniforms, eating cod instead of catfish, wielding billy clubs instead of cattle prods.

And so here we are.

We have tried calling the cops. Ha hah. Calling the cops.

We know the justifications are excuses. We know the lies are lies. We know we did not bring this on ourselves. We know we deserve better from this relationship, having built the house in which we live with our sweat and labor, having watered the fertile garden with tears and blood. We also know we deserve better treatment not only for those reasons but simply because we are human. But only a child believes people always get what they deserve.

"Black people will never gain full equality in this country," said Derrick Bell in a keynote address at the Howard University

School of Law in 1991. "Even those herculean efforts we hail as successful will produce no more than temporary 'peaks of progress,' short-lived victories that slide into irrelevance as racial patterns adapt in ways that maintain White dominance. This is a hard-to-accept fact that all history verifies. We must acknowledge it and move on."

Bell meant move *on*, not *move* on. But it makes one wonder.

On bad days, like the days when I came under sustained and public attack by racist, rightwing trolls—much more on that later—I think of all the great Black American writers, artists, activists and thinkers who fled the country of their birth. Richard Wright, James Baldwin, Chester Himes, Nina Simone, Augusta Savage, Jessie Fauset and many others left for France, which really says something. W.E.B. DuBois died a Ghanaian citizen after the American government refused to renew his passport; whether he would have chosen to return to the US from Ghana had he been allowed is unknown. Stokely Carmichael exiled himself to Guinea. Tina Turner died in Zurich.

What does it say that so many thoughtful, observant, insightful people—people who saw things clearly, people not susceptible to myths and make believe, not inclined toward magical thinking about the arc of justice bending inevitably one way, people who used their considerable intelligence and energy and gifts trying to urge, persuade and compel America to do the right thing— what does it say that so many of these people eventually gave up on America? What does it mean that those who could shook their heads and clasped their hearts and fled?

～

On Veteran's Day my brother sends out a text to the family group chat: *Happy Veteran's Day to my fellow vets. I am proud of you and your service. We keep loving this country even though this country doesn't love us back.* Literally the same words as Doc Rivers. *Thank you for your service,* I type. I should just leave it at that, *know* I should just shut up and fold my hands. But the writer's job, Baldwin taught me, is to challenge the fallback, to push and keep pushing, to question the dream. *But why?* I text. *Why keep loving if you are not only not loved in return but actively abused?* Across the miles I feel the collective roll of eyes. No one responds.

～

It took an embarrassingly long time for me to finally extricate myself from my post-divorce dysfunctional relationships, but eventually I did. Importantly, I faced no physical danger in leaving, which cannot be said for those in truly abusive relationships; all I had to do was finally decide I'd had enough. Still, the point remains: the only surefire way to end the abuse in an abusive relationship is to get away from the abuser. The only sure thing to do, despite the

69

difficulty and the danger, is to leave.

Here is where our metaphor, already overburdened and quivering, collapses beneath the strain. It's going to be very difficult to find a safe place for forty-eight million people. There is no shelter for us. Wakanda does not seem to exist; if it does, the borders are decidedly closed. Liberia? Ghana? (The country's "The Year of Return" in 2019 was a marketing and tourism success, but tourism is not migration.) How about France, complicated haven to a generation of Black veterans, artists, and intellectuals?

Not France.

Can we all go together? Can we take our food and our language and our dances and our music and our fashion and our hairstyles and our churches and nightclubs and Black Twitter and sweet potato pies and "Lift Every Voice and Sing," and if we can't, isn't that just another diaspora, just a further fracturing?

Nor does everyone wish to leave. David Walker, writing in 1829 in *David Walker's Appeal to the Colored Citizens of the World*, dismissed the send-them-back-to-Africa plans of the American Colonization Society, urging his fellow Black Americans to resist the urge to flee: "Let no man of us budge one step, and let slave-holders come to beat us from our country. America is more our country, than it is the Whites'—we have enriched it with our *blood and tears*. The greatest riches in all America have arisen from our blood and tears: and will they drive us from our property and homes, which we have earned with our *blood?*"

My own family shrugs when I raise the idea of buying some

land abroad, establishing our own community somewhere. *No place is perfect,* they say. *Not hoping for perfection,* I respond. *Just less relentless, sustained brutality.* Again they shrug. They do not wish to give up. They do not want to leave. They love America.

Baldwin famously fled the country when he was only twenty-four, but returned when he had become *James Baldwin* and spent the rest of his life crossing back and forth. Unlike some—Wright, Baker, Simone—he never severed the relationship completely, never walked away with no intention to return. His family was here, and his people. His responsibility as a witness and an artist. Anyway, walking away is never really walking away. In an interview with John Romano published in *The New York Times* in September 1979, Baldwin said, "I discovered, quite literally, that you carry your home with you. There is no way you can escape from it—to think otherwise is simply an illusion."

Still, Baldwin knew enough to keep a safe emotional distance from his abuser. In the many, many hours of his speeches, interviews and talks about America that I have watched, I've seen him alternately icy and angry, sometimes bewildered, sometimes weary and resigned. But I've never seen a clip of Baldwin openly broken-hearted. He never cries.

My fellow Black Americans, it may be necessary to remain in this country but it is not necessary to keep loving it. An abusive relationship can take your trust, your sense of safety, even your life. What the abuser cannot take—what you don't have to give— is your heart.

On Being Anti-White,
and Other Lies

I'm in a meeting in the middle of the day when the provost calls, which is strange. The provost does not often call. If she needs to reach me, email is the preferred medium, or she can just walk down the hall. Why would she be phoning me midday on a Tuesday? Why does she sound so concerned when I answer? Why does she ask if I'm on campus? Is she checking up on me? Boy, am I glad I came in today.

But, no, she's not calling to check up; she's calling because a bomb threat has just been received, and I am the target. Me and another employee of the institution, a woman who is also Black. The college police have been alerted, and are looking into it, but the provost thinks I should leave campus immediately. I agree. I begin gathering my things, trying to explain to the other people present what is happening. "A bomb threat against me," is a weird thing to say.

I skip the elevator and head for the stairwell, mostly out of habit but also because it seems like a good idea. Never get on an elevator during a fire. Never get on an elevator during a bomb threat. Bomb threat, bomb threat, bomb threat. Later it will occur to me that had the threat been a ruse to smoke me out, the elevator might have been the wiser choice. Terrorists don't take elevators, do they? Terrorists always take the stairs.

Outside, people stroll along the sidewalks, enjoying the sunny day. Ours is an urban campus, located in the heart of historic Boston and on this crystalline late spring day the tourists are out in force, phones and maps in hand. *This way to the Freedom Trail! See where America was born!* The sight of the throngs calms me. I always feel safer in cities; on a crowded city street the numbers and diversity of human beings are on your side. Sure, there may be people who hate you but there is also likely to be someone who would come to your aid. (It's the suburbs which scare me, not to mention the countryside.) But waiting for the light to change it occurs to me that perhaps the threat (*bomb threat, bomb threat, bomb threat*) was really just a trick to lure me outside. Maybe the terrorist is lingering nearby, stalking our buildings, waiting for me to show myself. Moving closer as the cars race past, cradling his American gun.

The provost had suggested I contact the college police for an escort to my car. Later, when I tell the story, many of my White colleagues will wonder why I didn't demand such an escort, why an officer was not immediately dispatched. This faith in the system strikes me as touching; like the person who later assures me the FBI will get to the bottom of the threat.

The provost's suggestion for a police escort had gone in one ear and out the other before I even hung up the phone. For one thing, I took public transportation to work. An officer could possibly have escorted me to the nearest train stop, but besides drawing unwanted attention to myself, this would have required either waiting for an officer to arrive or walking to the building where the public safety office is housed—in which case I might as well just walk to the train. More critically, while our campus chief strikes me as a kind and thoughtful man, it is against my instinct to turn to the police in times of crisis. In truth, I don't trust the cops to keep me safe.

Alone, I head for the train station. The closest stop is one block away but I usually, seeking exercise, catch the train further along. So out of habit I head down Boylston Street, getting in my steps. Along the busy Boston Common. Through the lovely Public Garden. Down the shop-fronted sidewalks, scanning passing tourists and passing cars for people who want to take my life. After a few blocks I feel safe enough to call my husband. I tell him what is happening. *I'm fine, don't leave work,* I say, though I know he will.

Aboard the train I check my email, find warnings from colleagues in other offices who have seen the threat. I ask one such colleague to call, and when she does, I press for details. While I remember talking to this colleague, I can't recall if I asked her to forward the threat, which came by email, or if she did or didn't, or if I actually read it or not. My brain has a very helpful habit of blocking out stuff like that.

I just remember standing on the train, looking out the dirty window at the passing city, wondering if this was the way things were going to be from here on out. I remember feeling sorry for myself, thinking it was all so absurd and outrageous and unfair. I remember feeling afraid and not wanting to feel afraid. I remember wanting only to feel pissed.

~

I don't remember the first time someone accused me of hating White people. This blank spot is interesting to me: I would have thought the moment so jarring it lodged permanently in mind, like the first time someone called me a nigger. If forced to guess, I'd say the first time someone accused me of being anti-White was high school, because high school, while not my first introduction to White people, was my introduction to both the spoils and the tantrums of White supremacy.

In my integrated elementary and junior high schools the White kids were generally, but not exclusively, better off economically than the Black kids; regardless, I was top of the class academically and so did not really care. But at the elite, overwhelmingly-White New England boarding school where I ended up as a scholarship student, I struggled academically and emotionally. White students and faculty questioned my presence and my intelligence, linking both to the color of my skin. This was when I began to really understand that White people felt themselves better than me—and also to see clearly how ridiculous that was. High school was when I began speaking up against White supremacy.

I know it happened in college, when I wrote a story for the campus newspaper critiquing the ideology of colorblindness and asking for an honest grappling with campus racism. It happened again when I complained of the backlash to a White guy I was dating. And when I critiqued American exceptionalism in history class.

It happened again in the years after college, as I worked as a journalist in North Carolina and Philadelphia and New York. Sometimes the accusation was direct and unflinching. Other times, as when a city councilman complained to the editor about my critical coverage, it was merely implied. At a book signing for my first novel a man in the audience accused the mother character, a Black woman from Jim Crow Mississippi who is suspicious of White people, of being racist.

"She's just as bad as my grandfather who hates all Black people," he said. "It's all the same."

I disagreed, pointing out the mother character, like my own mother, came of age in a place and time where White people had the state-supported right to order her off the sidewalk, and to lynch her if she did not comply. Her suspicion of White people was utterly rational, I explained. His grandfather, on the other hand, was just a racist.

The man was furious. *Oh, you hate White people!*

Well, now, let's look at this.

"The crisis of leadership in the White community is remarkable and terrifying because there is, in fact, no White community," wrote James Baldwin. "This may seem an enormous statement and it is. I am willing to be challenged. I'm also willing to attempt to spell it out." The quote comes from the essay "On Being White . . . and Other Lies" in which Baldwin makes the irrefutable (and yet still debated) point that there was no such thing as White people at the "founding" of what became the United States of America. The people who stepped off the Mayflower onto the shores of Plymouth, Massachusetts, did not consider themselves White, identifying as Englishmen and/or Christians. Whiteness as a racial category was a necessary and deliberate creation of the slave-based economies of the English Caribbean and North America, put in place over time, decision by decision, law by law, brick by brick,[1] in order to justify the theft of land, the genocide of Indigenous people and, most critically, the enslavement of Africans.

As historian Katharyn Gerbner writes,[2] before 1700, religion, not skin color, was the crucial difference between

---

1. "Selected Virginia Statutes Relating to Slavery." Virtual Jamestown: Indentured Servants, www.virtualjamestown.org/slavelink.html.
2. Gerbner, Katharine. "Most People Think 'Whiteness' Is Innate. They're Wrong: It Was Created to Keep Black People from Voting." *The Washington Post*, April 27, 2018. https://www.washingtonpost.com/news/made-by-history/wp/2018/04/27/most-people-think-whiteness-is-innate-theyre-wrong-it-was-created-to-keep-black-people-from-voting/.

slavery and freedom. Indentured servants from Europe could be mistreated, exploited and abused but, as Christians, could not be held in perpetual servitude. Africans, on the other hand, could be treated like the "infidels" they were deemed to be. But when, despite intense slave owner opposition, Africans began pressing for, and winning, baptism in English Protestant churches, things got messy. If they were Christians, they could no longer be enslaved. And if a baptized man of African descent, such as Olauduah Equiano, not only gained his freedom but acquired property, he could claim his right not only to vote but to hold government office, and use both to push for the abolition of slavery. This was a big enough problem, but add to it the specter of landless or small-farming Europeans making common cause with indentured or enslaved Africans against the exploitation of the wealthy and the elite (see Bacon's Rebellion[3]) and suddenly you have yourself a real threat to the slaveowning class.

What to do, what to do? Brainstorm: create Whiteness, and its twin White supremacy.[4]

It would be untrue to say I knew this history when I was

---

3. Mark, Joshua J. "Bacon's Rebellion." *World History Encyclopedia.* March 3, 2021. https://www.worldhistory.org/Bacon%27s_Rebellion..

4. Baird, Robert P. "The Invention of Whiteness: The Long History of a Dangerous Idea." *The Guardian*, April 20, 2021. https://www.theguardian.com/news/2021/apr/20/the-invention-of-Whiteness-long-history-dangerous-idea.

sixteen or eighteen or twenty, the first time someone accused me of being anti-White. Despite what might be considered an excellent education (Phillips Exeter Academy, Duke University) I had not encountered Frederick Douglass, Harriet Jacobs, Ida B. Wells, Richard Wright, Langston Hughes, Du Bois, Locke, Malcolm, Morrison or Baldwin, to name a few, and so although I had long begun questioning the meaning and impact of Blackness, questioning the meaning and impact of Whiteness had not occurred to me. I lacked the political language to describe what I was resisting, could not precisely articulate the structural nature of the problem. I could not yet say, as Baldwin said, that Whiteness is "a moral choice." But I saw. And I knew.

I was sixteen years old when Ronald Regan launched his presidential campaign by lauding states' rights in Philadelphia, Mississippi, within walking distance of the muddy hole where three Civil Rights workers had been unceremoniously dumped by their murderers in 1964. Seventeen when he used his racist "welfare queen" mythologizing to slash public benefits to low-income children while handing tax breaks to the rich. Eighteen when he vetoed sanctions against apartheid in South Africa, and twenty when White America rewarded him with a second term. I was twenty-two when the Anti-Drug Abuse Act of 1986 created wide disparities between federal penalties for crack versus cocaine possession. Twenty-eight when I covered the Los Angeles riots in the wake of the acquittal of the police who mercilessly beat Rodney King, which Black folk across America knew was an anomaly only for being caught on tape. I was in my thirties when predatory lending aimed at Black and Brown neighborhoods laid the foundation for the 2008 housing crisis. This list could go on and on. I saw all this, and spoke about them, sometimes angrily, sometimes with dismay, and the response from my White colleagues and my White in-laws and, finally, my White husband was: *Oh, you hate White people.*

Accusations of anti-Whiteness from strangers surprised and sometimes rankled, but accusations of anti-Whiteness from colleagues and family never failed to bewilder and sting. Didn't these people know me? Didn't they know my heart? Or, you know, failing that, had they not, at least, read some of my work? As a journalist I covered both the impact of systematic racism in North Philadelphia and the impact of the oppression and domination of indigenous Africans by the colonizing formerly enslaved freedmen (i.e. Americo-Liberians) who landed on their shores in West Africa. I wrote about a White neo-Nazi murderer and a Black mother who beat her four-year-old daughter to death with an extension cord. I wrote novels about a flawed White man and the flawed Black woman he loved. Had I ever labored under the illusion that American White supremacy was rooted in some kind of inherent evilness in people whose skin is pale, instead of in historical patterns of power and domination—had I ever been naive enough to believe such a thing then life as a working journalist, not to mention the concurrent study of history, would have relieved me of such belief.

Accusations of anti-Whiteness from White people who knew me were also bewildering because—let's be frank—my life was steeped in Whiteness. The schools I'd attended; the neighborhoods in which I lived; the man I dated and eventually married and many of my closest friends were White. The first two churches I joined as an adult were White, though with a patina of integration; not until my children were born did I make an effort to find a progressive Black church. Even as I was being accused of hating White people I was spending far more time among them than among Black people—not to mention far more time than my accusers spent outside their White cocoon. So much of my life during my twenties and thirties was spent among White people that the secret fear simmering in my heart during those years was that what I really hated was Blackness. This is the far bigger danger for any Black person growing up in America. This is the far bigger threat.

Listen: White supremacy will get you coming and going, outside and inside, today, tomorrow and yesterday if you let it, if it can.

That shit is wild.

❧

But, oh, the living look at you

with human eyes whose suffering accuses you,
whose hatred reaches through the swill of dark
to strike you like a leper's claw.

You cannot stare that hatred down
or chain the fear that stalks the watches
and breathes on you its fetid scorching breath;
cannot kill the deep immortal human wish,
the timeless will.

—"Middle Passage" by Robert Hayden

Accusations of anti-Whiteness go back as far as Black resistance to White oppression and supremacy. David Walker, the fearless and prophetic author, was accused of being motivated not by the desire to end slavery but by hatred of White people. A man identified as "V" wrote in the April 1831 edition of the anti-slavery paper *The Liberator* that:

I have often heard, and constantly believed, that Walker's Appeal was the incoherent rhapsody of a blood-thirsty, but vulgar and very ignorant fanatic . . . I have now read the book and my opinions are changed . . . I am convinced that he was a brave, just, good man, endowed with talents of no mean order, deeply and properly persuaded of the wrongs of his race . . . It is vain to call him incendiary, ruffian, or exciter of sedition . . .

Frederick Douglass spent years debating critics of his famous 1845 *Narrative of the Life of Frederick Douglass, An American Slave,* slapping down not only charges of exaggeration, falsehoods and misrepresentation but of "unwarranted" hatred of White slave owners. The Reverend Ephraim Peabody unfavorably compared Douglass to the authors of several other slave narratives, who told their stories of woe "without noise or pretension, without bitterness toward the whites, without extravagant claims on behalf of the blacks." George Graham, writing in the January 1853 edition of *Graham's Magazine* (and you thought Oprah started that trend!) contended that although he respected Douglass, "we hate the present negro literature— especially that of Fred's, which by abusing the white, is intended to elevate the black man . . . while the very bitterness and rancor shown in their writings, and their almost infernal rage for making money out of moral questions, prove them to be fully as much the children of Satan as any they rebuke."

It is no surprise that Malcolm X—firebrand and demagogue, a self-made and remade man motivated by a pulsing love for his people—was accused of anti-White hatred, but it may surprise some that the Reverend Dr. Martin Luther King Jr. was likewise accused, as were Ida B. Wells, Angela Davis and of course, James Baldwin. And the greatest American intellectual of the twentieth century, William W.E.B. Du Bois, upon publishing his groundbreaking work, *Darkwater,* was accused in *The Kansas*

City Times of "stirring up race hatred." A reviewer for *The Daily News* called Du Bois a 'raving madman' and his book a "hymn of hate." Margaret Emerson Bailey, reviewing for *The Bookman,* compared *Darkwater* to a rant by the White nationalist and eugenicist Lothrop Stoddard, writing that, ". . . while Mr. Stoddard enters the fray from fear, from the basic instinct of self-preservation, Mr. Du Bois seeks out the contest prompted by resentment *and by hate.*" Emphasis mine.

Well. The best defense of the indefensible is a self-righteous offense. See defenders of patriarchy in South Korea accuse people pushing for gender equity of being man-haters. See importers of Indian caste bias into US tech firms accuse advocates for Dalit equality of being anti-Hindu. See defenders of Israeli oppression and displacement of Palestians accuse anyone who objects to this treatment of being anti-Semitic. And on and on.

In the field of domestic violence, this tactic is called DARVO. Based on the work of psychologist Jennifer Freyd, DARVO is an acronym laying out a common strategy practiced by abusers when confronted with their abuse: deny, attack, reverse victim and offender.

Another word for this is gaslighting.

I remember the first time I saw the movie from which the phrase originates. A fragile Ingrid Bergman. An oily Charles Boyer. A dull-as-dishwater Joseph Cotten and an ending filled with classic suspense. But the scene which chilled me the most comes earlier in the film. After months of subterfuge by

Boyer—flickering lights, unidentifiable noises, disappearing objects—Bergman's psyche is battered but not broken: she still resists her husband's insistence that she is mentally unstable. Fighting the isolation he has imposed, one night she insists on attending a concert. Boyer decides to use the opportunity for a public humiliation; in the middle of the concert he pulls his watch from her purse, driving home his depiction of her as a kleptomaniac disassociated from her own actions. Back home a dazed Bergman fights to hold on to her sense of reality, remembering that his accusations began the day she found a letter to her aunt from Sergis Bauer, the real name of Boyer's character. Threatened by the near revelation of his secret, Boyer attacks, using one last deception to tip Bergman over the edge. She lets go of what she knows to be true, breaking as she accepts her husband's declared version of reality.

Accusations of anti-Whiteness are gaslighting. They know it's bullshit and you know it's bullshit, but the balance of power is on their side. If other people (Angela Lansberry's maid) join in the deception, they can persuade the persuadable others that the insanity is progressing, that you are the problem, that the solution is to shut you down or put you away. And, if you're not careful, they can make you believe it, too.

The first time someone accused me of hating White people, I lacked both the political language to accurately define what I was resisting and the psychological language to define the accusation itself. I knew that what I felt was not hatred but opposition, and that the target was something big and structural and created, not individuals whose skin happened to be lighter than mine. This saved me from breaking. But I'd be lying if I said I didn't fear that others would believe this lie about me. I'd be lying if I said the accusations didn't hurt.

Which is funny. Because there's also this: if I *actually* did hate White people, it would not be unreasonable. Regrettable, perhaps. Dangerous to my own sanity and soul. But not unreasonable, unfounded, unsound. If any Black person, knowing not only the full history of American White supremacy but, more importantly, the very real ways in which this foundational doctrine continues to touch everything from infant mortality to student discipline to mass incarceration to housing appraisals to whether or not I'll get pain medication or aggressive coronary treatment in the emergency room—if, knowing all this, any conscious Black person actually did hate White people, who in the natural world could blame them, except "White people?"

What's amazing is how few Black people carry such hatred, nor even the desire for separation, disconnection, distance. Garveyism, the Nation of Islam, the Black Panther Party for Self-Defense—none of these Black nationalist groups were, at base, anti-White and yet not even at their most popular did they attract more than a minority of Black Americans. Compare that to the majority of White Americans who voted for Donald Trump, who supported and endorsed his racism, who continue to support some unholy combination of The Big Lie/QAnon/ Proud Boys, etc. Why are White Americans more prone to political extremism than Black Americans? Why is it easier for White people today to believe in "White replacement theory" than for Black people in the 1950s, scanning legal segregation, Black impoverishment and the terrorist violence of Jim Crow, to believe White people were created in a test tube by a mad scientist? Is it because Whiteness is a delusion that not only enables but requires other delusions?

Including the comforting delusion of anti-Whiteness.

∾

The congratulatory flowers were still on the table when the shit hit the fan. I hadn't even changed the water yet.

This was six months before the bomb threat, and it had just been announced that I was being appointed interim dean of graduate and professional studies. This was not a position I sought, but it was one I accepted. Not knowing what was to come.

It was a Saturday afternoon. I checked my email (serves me right for checking work email on the weekend) and found a missive from someone identifying himself as a reporter for a Boston publication of which I had never heard. He was writing a story about my promotion, and about my clear anti-Whiteness. He linked to several of my essays as proof and asked if I would care to comment.

My husband and I were about to dress for a dinner party with friends, a pleasant outing at which, ironically but not unusually, I would be the only person not White. Stomach clenching, I read the email to my husband. Then he told me I had received a different but similar email at my website, which he monitored. He had not liked the tone and so had just ignored the email, not wanting to worry me. I asked him to forward the message, which turned out to include almost the same language, though a bit harsher, from another "reporter" planning a story. Two different reporters, two different outlets, both preparing stories within hours of one another. Obviously not a coincidence.

I forwarded the email to the interim provost and the college counsel, apologizing for bringing the wolves to their door. It's astonishing to me now, but the truth is that the first emotion to sweep over me that day was not fear but guilt. We were all about to go through a shitstorm at a time the college was already struggling and it would all be my fault, not for writing what I wrote, but for accepting the promotion. Immediately I began kicking myself. I should never have said yes to the offer. I should have stayed where I was, below the glance of the Evil Eye.

But although guilt arrived first, fear soon followed. I knew damn well what happened to Black people and to women—and especially to Black women—who drew the attention of rightwing hate mobs. I knew exactly how ugly and frightening things could get. I set about making myself as small a target as possible. Thanking God that months before, even before the job offer arrived, I had purged my Twitter account and began being more careful about what I posted on Instagram, I immediately deactivated both accounts. I took my blog offline and asked my husband to close the comments and email sections on my website, and to screen both my work and private email accounts. Essentially I went into a defensive crouch.

Later, as the college worked to come up with a response plan for future such attacks, the head of IT security would ask me how I knew to respond as I had. Many people would not have been able to act so quickly and decisively. What had driven me? "Instinct," I told him then, but I think a better answer might be: blood memory. The minute I received that first email I knew the dogs had been released. I could hear them baying through the woods, knew they had my scent. I had to run and I had to do it immediately. "When your back is pressed to the wall you go to the deepest part of yourself, and there's a response," said August Wilson. "It's your great ancestors talking. It's blood memory."

We shut down my digital life then went to the dinner party. The first hate mail would have arrived by the time we got home but for the bulk of the evening I managed to put on a game face, chatting about kids and sports and vacations to France. Not until someone asked about my work did the story come out. Along with the tears.

"There's just jerks," said one guy. "Fuck 'em."

"Don't let the bastards get you down," said another man.

This was a generous response of support and I was touched by it. But as the barrage continued over the next few weeks, as the hate mail and threats continued, I would hear some version of that line repeated over and over again: *Stay strong, don't quit, don't let the bastards win.* Mostly this was said by White people. Black people, in general, said: *I'm sorry, that sucks, are you okay?* But one young Black woman, a student, reached out kindly to offer support and, when I responded with my thanks and some honest comment about wanting to give up and leave this country, reminded me of how much harder it was for our ancestors, how much more they had to fight and bleed and die. Didn't I owe it to them to keep fighting? Couldn't I—shouldn't I—do the same?

Well, now, I guess that depends. I'm nearly sixty. I've been speaking and writing and protesting and advocating since I was sixteen and, as far as I can tell, the vast majority of Americans whose skin happens to be pale are no closer to an honest reckoning with Whiteness, no closer to dismantling, or even really wanting to dismantle, White supremacist capitalist hetero-patriarchy (ht bell hooks) than they were the first time someone accused me of being anti-White.

It's one thing to keep fighting when you believe in the possibility of change. But what if the bastards have already won?

PART TWO

On Being

Everyday Something Has Tried
to Kill Me and Has Failed

"Don't get old," my mother says as I dry her back. It's not the first time she has issued this warning, not even the first time today. Rolling out of bed to take her morning meds she reached for her cane, pushed herself to her feet, gave me a little smile. "Don't get old."

Helping her on with her shirt, I remind my mother that I have already breezed passed fifty, am well along the path to no longer being young. Old age is coming for me sooner than I would like to consider, sooner than either one of us would like to believe. She looks startled at my reminder: how is it possible to have a child over the age of fifty, already nearing retirement? How is it possible to have lived so long?

She never expected to live this long.

"Don't get old," my mother says. Sometimes, making my voice high and light, I leap in to finish her thought: "It's not for wimps, huh?"

"It's not for wimps," my mother confirms. By "wimp" she means someone who lacks the strength to do the tough, unpleasant job at hand. Strength of that kind is not a thing my mother has ever lacked, having been handed many tough and unpleasant jobs during her life, not the least of which was raising five children all alone. She is the toughest person I have ever known and also the most fragile, unbreakable but easily fractured, prone to chips and cracks and dents. I keep trying to find the right metaphor, a way of capturing a woman who is the opposite of those White southern women they call steel magnolias. My mother is one of those Black southern women who grew armor in order to survive a hostile world but remained inside as fragile as a robin's egg. A shelter built with crepe paper. A tank of woven spider webs. A fortress spun from glass. Something like that.

We finish her shower, an exhausting fifteen minutes for her, no pleasure, all chore. She prefers baths but climbing in and out of the tub now is dangerous. I rinse out the stall while she shuffles down the hall to put her dirty clothes in the washing machine. I could do this for her but it is important that she contribute to the running of the household, that she continue to do things for herself. When I first arrived, visiting after more than a year away due to Covid, I tried to do everything, running around the house in a frenzy, waiting on her hand and foot, until she said, "I feel so useless" and I stopped.

I do not visit enough.

My mother lives with my sister on the other side of the country, the other side of the continent. I take off over the

Atlantic and land over the Pacific and drive a rental car to my sister's house. There are five of us, four girls and one boy, but my sister has taken on the burden of caring for our mother alone. The rest of us try to help when and how we can but it is inadequate. It is all inadequate.

Don't get old.

I make lunch: yogurt for me, a turkey sandwich for my mother, strips of meat on bread as soft and white as drifts of snow. The kind of bread I grew up eating and now, in my East Coast arrogance, disdain. My mother loves it still, and, anyway, her teeth will not accommodate the hearty multigrain or crusty baguette I prefer, because, in America, poor people don't deserve dental care. To the tray I add a small salad drenched in Thousand Island dressing, some chunks of watermelon and cantaloupe, a Snapple iced tea. She takes her noontime pills, four of them including vitamins. She has already taken a handful of other meds after breakfast and will take another handful before bed, more pills in one day than I take in months.

We watch *The People's Court* or, more likely, *Judge Judy*, shows which make me simultaneously feel better about my life and despair for humanity. What I know about Judge Judy is that she's been on forever and made a ton of money and likes to berate people and thinks herself very tough and very discerning and very smart, which, compared to the people who come before her in her "courtroom," she certainly is. It's funny how people often confuse being in the right place at the right time with deserving what they luck into, but I will give Judy this: she has spawned an infestation of imitators. Every time I visit my mother (the only time I watch daytime television), I discover another court show: Judge Matthis (a buffoonish, jive-shucking, Black man,) Judge Faith, Judge Jeanie, not to mention *Divorce Court*, and, astonishingly, *Paternity Court*. Even Jerry Springer got to play judge for fun and profit in America before he died. Everything about these shows seems petty and grimy and small, a relentless parade of accusation and humiliation and delusion. Especially delusion; people lying to others, and, time after relentless time, to themselves. When I ask my mother why she likes these shows she shrugs and laughs. The perfect response.

"Put on Dr. Pimple Popper," she says. Meaning, *if you think that's something, watch this. Dr. Pimple Popper,* which I have never seen and which I cannot quite believe actually exists, is a reality show in which a pretty young Asian dermatologist meets people with all kinds of horrible, disfiguring skin conditions, talks gently to them about the impact of the hideous growths on their lives and self-esteem and then proceeds to, yes, pop the pimple or pare the keloid or surgically remove the lipoma the size of a tennis ball dangling on the inside of their leg, all of this on camera, blood and pus and stitches and all. I am sickened but my mother watches with fascination. "Isn't that amazing?" she says. "Don't you think that's interesting?"

She wanted, at one time, to be a nurse.

When the pimple show is over I dig out a checkerboard from the cabinet. The last time I visited I tried to get my mother interested in puzzles, in Sudoku, in embroidery. No dice. I long ago gave up trying to interest her in reading, gave up trying to understand why our childhood home was full of books she never opened. I opened them. They set me on my path.

My sister has also given up trying to get our mother to write her memoir. "I wouldn't want to depress people," my mother says when I ask again. Six months later, when I visit again, she will have forgotten that she was opposed. "I was going to write a book about my life but I can't remember it. My memory is so bad."

She wanted, at one time, to be a writer.

She says yes to the checkers, though, mostly to shut me up, I think. I plan to go easy on her, but, after listening to my refresher of the rules, my mother quickly captures half my men, lands three kings, then captures the rest of my pieces. I am surprised and delighted and a little chagrined, the competitive instinct being what it is; it's like the first time your child beats you in something fair and square. I ask if she wants to play again. She shakes her head.

"I'm trying to remember what I did with all my time," she says.

"What do you mean?"

"I didn't play checkers, never liked to play card games. I was not a big reader. I'm trying to remember what I did with all my time."

"You worked," I say. "You worked hard."

She nods. "Working outside the house or working inside the house. No time for myself."

Rocking herself to her feet the way the physical therapist taught her, my mother grabs her cane and heads upstairs to nap.

~

I used to think I had a pretty good grip on aging, that I understood and accepted the inevitable. I would not be one of those people who go around saying things like, "Age is nothing but a number" (yes, and so is miles per hour and so is blood pressure and both those things will kill you if the number grows high enough so what exactly is your point?) or that fifty is the new thirty (it isn't) or that being around college students keeps one young (they exhaust me.) I would not be like the middle-aged men I dated post-divorce who described themselves as "just a big kid" and who, in fact, dressed like toddlers and acted like adolescents and labeled women their own age "yucky" but believed themselves to be magically, eternally youthful, men who at forty-five or forty-eight still wanted to settle down and have children "some day." I would not be ridiculous.

I believed my equanimity about aging came from not having loved childhood or adolescence that much. I was an odd, outsider child, an odd outsider teen. My twenties were full of confusion and yearning, my thirties a blur of depression and marriage and childrearing. A lot of stuff happened and a lot of stuff was accomplished but through most of it I felt like I was sleepwalking. At forty I stirred, my eyelids fluttered, light filtered in. At forty-five I sat up and looked around. I see. Okay.

Fifty I greeted not with dread but with exhilaration; I knew who I was, knew what I wanted and did not want and finally liked myself. I didn't fear losing my looks because I had grown up not thinking I had any. As a teen and young woman I thought myself fat and ugly; not until I was well over thirty did that hegemonic delusion subside. Somewhere around forty or maybe forty-five I realized that not only was I not ugly, I was actually pretty damn attractive, even beautiful. (Around this time my niece, doing a project for some college class, asked me how "pretty privilege" had impacted my life. I started to protest that I never *felt* pretty but stopped when she raised an eyebrow. Not being consciously aware of privilege does not negate its power. For that brief moment I felt like a White person.) For a time this realization made me sad; in some ways, though not others, youth was wasted on me. Had I known I was beautiful I would have cut through the world of men like a warrior, instead of sneaking around like a beggar seeking alms. But girls who come to womanhood valued for their beauty can learn to lean on that beauty like a cane, atrophying the muscles needed to stand upright. I came to womanhood believing that my brain and not my face would be the source of my salvation. My brain was myself.

This was a gift, in the long run. At fifty my face was wrinkling, my body softening, beginning to sag. But my brain was stronger than ever. My brain—well constructed, meticulously maintained—was firing on all cylinders, free from the gummy oil of youthful obliviousness and ruinous self-doubt. I threw myself a fiftieth birthday party: three cakes, two changes of outfit, sixty people roaming my house and me not giving a damn. I played the music I wanted and ate the food I wanted and talked to whoever held my interest until they didn't. I danced and danced and danced. I was not afraid of turning fifty; I was liberated.

Sweeping the living room the day after the party, I realized I had no memory of my mother at fifty, this new and wonderful age. Had no memory of her taking a step back and surveying her life with satisfaction, no memory of her coming happily into herself. In my memory, my mother is first young, harried and beautiful and then suddenly, one day, she is old. What explains this abrupt transition? Part of it, probably was my own selfishness. During those middle years of my mother's life I was preoccupied, focused on my work and my depression and my marriage and my children and my own monkey mind. I checked in on her from a distance, both geographically and emotionally. I thought the best thing I could do for my mother was not to add to her considerable burdens, either financially or emotionally. By leaving her alone I was helping her. So I told myself.

So my navel-gazing probably explains part of this, as does

the fact that in her sixties my mother developed a serious illness, one I believe was caused in part by the stress of her life. But even before that illness my mother seemed older than she actually was. Older than my ex mother-in-law, for example, though she was, in fact, younger. Older than a White woman friend from my church. Sometimes people ask my mother's age. In the first part of your life people ask you how old you are, then they ask the age of your children, finally they ask the age of your parents, if your parents are still alive. Sometimes people ask my mother's age and I give it, followed by a qualification. *She's eighty-three, but it's really more like 120. She's eighty-four and it's amazing she's still alive because life for her has been no crystal stair. She's eighty-five but it's a hard eighty-five.*

Some people age like trees, well-tended and watered. A tree grows from seed to sprout to sapling to mature to elderly to snag. Most trees spent the bulk of their years in maturity, bearing fruit or acorns or pecans or pine cones, seeking only to reproduce themself. Left alone, certain species of oaks can produce for 300 years before spending another 300 in a gentle decline toward death.

Some people age like animals, each year compressed. Some people's years are like animal years not because those people are "animals" (well, all people are animals but you know what I mean here) but because of the way they are treated by life. Some people age like trees because they live in a forest and some people age like animals because their world is a zoo.

~

A woman I know had a stroke recently. Eleven years younger than myself, perfectly healthy, no warning signs of any kind. She survived, thank God, but the road back to recovery is long. At least three women my age I know have high blood pressure. Another has fibroids so painful and debilitating she needed surgery. Another woman I know takes drugs to curb her compulsive hair-pulling, a painful and complex disorder that probably results from a combination of genetic and environmental causes. I could go on.

Strokes can happen to anyone. John Fetterman, the White senator from Pennsylvania, had a stroke, as did two sitting senators from New Mexico and Maryland. Strokes can happen to anyone but strokes happen to Black people far more often than to other people in America. Black people have the highest death rate from stroke of any racial group, and Black women are twice as likely as White women to have a stroke. Black men are 70 percent more likely to die of stroke than White men.

Seventy damn percent.

There are physical risk factors of course: weight, diabetes, long Covid. But every Black person in America knows the biggest risk to their health by far is the simple fact of being Black. Or, more accurately, being Black in a society undergirded by interlocking systems of oppression, what the writer and scholar bell hooks aptly summed up as "imperialist white supremacist heteropatriarchy." Let's call it IWSHP for short.

Even setting aside the question of how IWSHP collides with epigenetics (if people whose mothers were pregnant with them during the Dutch Winter Famine of 1944 were more likely than others to develop conditions like diabetes and heart disease, how could anyone doubt that gestating toward life under the wide-ranging impacts of structural racism impacts a fetus' health), living under the weight of IWSHP creates a stress that is real and cumulative and, for far too many of us, ultimately, untenable, a stress that is without question worse for those trapped at the bottom of the ladder but felt even by those at the top—ask Serena Williams. I grew up poor but since college have lived an economically stable, even privileged, middle-class life. Still, I wonder that I survived the depression of my twenties and thirties. Still there are days I return home inexplicably weary, barely able to make it through the door. For three or four weeks right around the time I learned of my friend's stroke, I found myself walking around exhausted, as though carrying the weight of the world. At the same time, I chided myself for feeling this way. There was no discernible reason; I spend my days sitting in meetings and fending off emails, not out chopping cotton under the glare of a White man on horseback. (Though sometimes reading newspaper articles about Black men out chopping cotton under the glare of White men on horseback. Hello Louisiana, my old friend.)

Finally I said to a friend, a Black woman from London. "I'm so tired and I don't know why. What's wrong with me?"

She said, "Weathering is real."

Maybe the reason I am a writer is because I find such power in words, in naming the unnamed. All Black women are indebted to researcher Arline T. Geronimus, who proposed the weathering hypothesis in 1992. She was trying to explain why Black women had better pregnancy outcomes in their late teens than in their mid-twenties, while White women, by contrast, faced a much lower risk of pregnancy complications in their mid-twenties than in their teens. The answer was this: the toxic stew of racism and sexism (misogynoir) in which Black women simmer from the day we are born takes a toll on our bodies, takes a toll on our health. Weathering.

Not everything is about race is such a funny thing for a White person to say to a Black person. I can't count how many times I've heard it. I can't count how many times I've rolled my eyes in response. Not everything is about race. Nobody wishes this were so more than Black people.

Here's an example. There's a critical long-term research study known as the Study of Women's Health Across the Nation, or SWAN. Since 1994, SWAN has been tracking the health of middle-aged women, becoming a major source of scientific knowledge about menopause and female health. But researchers at Stanford University decided to assess the original data set of potential participants, women forty-two to fifty-five, and found that many Black and Hispanic women had been excluded from the study early on. Why? Because the study was focused on pre-menopausal women and these women had already undergone menopause. But SWAN failed to account for the fact that Black and Hispanic women tend to undergo menopause earlier than White women. Why? Because of weathering.

Slotting these women back into the study (theoretically) produced some startling results. The average age at which women—regardless of race—experienced heart disease, hypertension, and diabetes was lowered by nearly twenty years. For Black and Hispanic women, insulin resistance, a precursor to diabetes, was found to begin eleven years earlier than the original SWAN data calculated, while heart disease, the number one killer of American women overall, began five years earlier. Meaning that by the time doctors, using the SWAN guidelines, begin screening us for these diseases, it may already be too late.

Not everything is about race. Weathering is real.

That same week my friend reminded me of weathering I read a story about Erica Gardner, the young woman who became a police reform activist after her father was choked to death by a NYC cop while crying, "I can't breathe." Three years later Erica Garner died of complications from a heart attack. She was twenty-seven. Her sister, Emerald Snipes Garner, described the stress of racism and White supremacy and police violence that took her sister's life: "They pull out one piece at a time, at a time, and another piece, and another piece, until you sort of collapse and you start losing pieces of your health and well-being."

"Weathering is real," said my friend.

"Yes," I responded. "Thank you for reminding me."

"War of attrition," she said.

Talking about weathering I felt oddly, immediately strengthened. The flip side of my depression has always been a certain stubbornness, the silver lining to the cloud. It's one thing to consider opting out of a world full of pain and unkindness, a world where, like it or not, bad things happen to good people and where, reports to the contrary, the assholes usually win. It is one thing to consider opting out of such a world, and another thing entirely to be driven from it. The idea of being killed by White supremacy at this late date is enough to get my Scottish up.

"I am not the victim here," said James Baldwin. Damn right.

Put another way: this is for colored girls who have considered suicide and might consider it still, but who sure as hell are not gonna let y'all take us out.

❧

A reporter, writing a story for Mother's Day, once asked me for the best piece of advice I ever received from my mother.

I am not a fan of Mother's Day, for many reasons I won't go into. Primarily, I dislike all days of consumerist obligation, sincerely fail to understand why receiving supermarket flowers or drug store chocolate on a day designated for such should make me feel special and thought about and loved. I told my husband early in our courtship that I didn't really need trinkets of affection but that if he was ever inspired to buy them anyway the one time he should absolutely resist the urge was Valentine's Day. Giving flowers on Valentine's Day, like going out on New Year's Eve, is for amateurs.

But my dislike of Mother's Day is not what stumped me at the reporter's question. It was the notion that my response would be printed alongside the answers of other "notable" women. I suspected—correctly as it turned out—that much of that advice would fall along the lines of "you can be anything you want to be" and "be kind to people" and "get up each day with a smile."

This was not the kind of advice my mother gave. Her advice tended more toward warnings of disaster, predictions of failure and doom. It usually came in the form of orders:

Get up. You can sleep when you're dead.

Don't get pregnant: it will ruin your life.

Nobody wants a nasty woman. (Nasty meaning both dirty and sexually promiscuous.)

I don't care what they called you. As long as those White people are not putting their hands on you, you stay up there with them and learn what they know.

All of this was wisdom in its way, just not the kind I longed for as a child. I wanted a mother who sat on my bunk bed (I wanted a bunk bed, desperately) and listened to my troubles and told me the sun would come up tomorrow and everything would be fine. I wanted a mother who kissed my forehead and told me she loved me. I wanted a mother who told me to get up each day with a smile.

Instead I got another kind of mother. And what's funny is that the mother I had was not the mother my siblings had. Ask each of us about our mother and you'll hear a completely different story, five blindfolded individuals describing an elephant. That made my mother several different people: the mother I wanted, the mother I had, the mother my siblings had and whoever she really was.

In old age my mother has become a different person than the mother of my childhood. Age and dementia have softened her; it's easier to forgive what one forgets. The grudges of a lifetime are at long last lost to memory, the anger and resentments finally released. Maybe that's what wisdom is: forgetting. Maybe my mother has grown wise. In old age and dementia my mother has finally let heal the wounds of childhood, wounds which festered all her life. She is loving, asking for a hug when I enter, another when I leave. She never mentions my father, and when the subject of an estranged relative comes up she just shakes her head and sighs. When I call her to tell her I made it home safely on the overnight flight she tells me she loves me, which rarely happened when I was young. In old age and dementia my mother has become the mother I always wanted. Or maybe it's truer to say she has become the mother I thought I wanted. So unlike the mother who shaped me. Who helped make me who I am.

~

A friend of mine used to lie awake at night terrified that her mother would die. That she would fear this as a child she understood, but the fear extended into adulthood, growing instead of diminishing, until by forty it was an all-consuming thing. Then one day a family secret came out, a secret held by her mother, a secret which reshaped my friend's understanding of herself. Suddenly the paralyzing fear of her mother dying disappeared. My friend feared the death of her mother because she sensed there was something she still needed from her, something valuable that had not yet been transferred but still could be. Both those things are key. I don't remember ever fearing the death of my mother. I must have, as a child, but I don't recall doing so. What my mother had to give me, which was nothing short of life, was long ago transferred.

Another friend who nursed his mother until she died says that tending an elderly person is a lot like tending a baby, except that with a baby the work is infused with promise and expectation and hope for the future while with an elderly person it is not. Raising children is about trying to correct for all the shortcomings of one's own childhood, to balm the wounds and ease the slights and fill the holes. Tending an elderly parent is about trying not to see that soon it will be you on the other side of the table, watching Judge Judy and waiting for your lunch.

It's amazing to me that people fear death more than this.

⁓

Six months after my last visit my mother's memory has worsened. She looks at the family photos hanging in her room and asks me who the people are. *That's your son. That's your daughter. That's one of your granddaughters. That one is you.* She refuses to believe the gray-haired woman with a cane and a mask is her, though I can't tell if this is true confusion or just the kind of disbelief that hits us all when confronted with evidence of our aging bodies. Last week I looked in the mirror and thought, "Not bad for your age!" Feeling cocky, I took a selfie. Big mistake. The mirror flatters and lies but the camera doesn't give a damn.

In my mother's room I pull out my phone and show her other pictures, pictures of her as a young woman, pictures of her beloved brother, now passed. She tries to tell me stories about her brother, stories I have heard a dozen times, but she can't remember the details and this frustrates her, even when I chime in. I redirect to stories of other relatives, great aunts and uncles she admired and loved. I ask about her mother, my grandmother, Iola. My mother doesn't want to talk about her mother. Some things are best left to fade.

After an hour of this I need a break, so I go downstairs to

the kitchen. Ten minutes later my mother is standing at the top of the stairs, calling plaintively: *Hello? Hello?* Afraid she has been abandoned. This becomes a pattern: one day all she wants to do is sleep, the next she is more awake and alert and does not want to be left alone. The challenge is to find something that will hold her interest. *You want to go outside? No, I don't like outside. Want to go for a ride? Not really. Want to play checkers? No. Read a book? No.* The day stretches on.

We watch television but few shows hold her interest. Even when one does, she finds following along challenging. Over and over she asks, "What did she say? What did he say?" My sister thought this was a hearing issue, and got my mother expensive hearing aids. But the questions continue even when the hearing aids are in and, anyway, she doesn't like wearing them, which I can understand. When is it too late for new things like hearing aids? When is it too late to try to make life better than it is?

Anyway, it's not just the dialogue. "What is she doing that for?" my mother asks, staring at *The Cosby Show.* "Who is that? Why is he walking that way?" The commercials are worse: "You ever heard of GoLo?" she asks. I say no but explain what it is. Fifteen minutes later the same commercial comes on and she asks again. And then again. It reminds me of when my children were young and constantly asking why, why, why. A preschool teacher told me it was normal for four-year-olds to ask as many as 300 questions a day as they tried to make sense of the world. Your job was to be patient and responsive and reassuring. Your job was not to let it set your teeth on edge.

I once knew a man who stopped visiting his mother in a nursing home because her dementia caused her to rage whenever she saw him. He could not bear the change from the soft, self-sacrificing mother he had always known. I knew a woman who blossomed in her declining years, enjoying a string of relationships with gentleman friends in her retirement village after her husband passed on. I know a woman who, at age ninety and in active congestive heart failure, eagerly seeks book recommendations and refuses to allow an oxygen machine in her home because it is "ugly." I know an imperfect woman who did imperfect things and heroic things and led a life that was both wide-ranging and painfully constrained and, who, toward the end, became a version of herself no one could have foreseen. There's no real way to predict what kind of old person a person will become. Not even oneself.

My mother is napping. I write her a note so she will not be frightened if she wakes and finds herself alone, then head out for a walk in the crystalline California sun. It feels good to walk, to still have use of my body, to feel competent. I hike a nearby hill, determined to not stop or slow down until I reach the top. Sometimes when walking I catch myself curling forward; when this happens I force myself to stand up straight, to lead with my hips instead of my shoulders, determined not to turn into one of those old people who walk with their face to the ground. Sometimes my knee throbs, but I ignore the pain. I have not bothered to see a doctor, not wanting a knee replacement. I am past the time of repair, focusing only for maintenance. My goal is limping out with the joints I brought in.

Don't get old, my mother says. I used to answer, "It beats the alternative!" It seemed the thing to say, the upbeat, encouraging way to beat back the pain behind my mother's words. Don't get old. *Sure but at least it's better than being dead! Being dead is worse than anything!*

I don't say that anymore.

When I go to wake my mother from her nap I ask if I can lower her bed, which is so high she needs a stepladder to climb into it. This is a falling hazard that frightens me but my mother likes to sleep high. Maybe for comfort. Maybe for safety. Maybe to be closer to God. She says no to my offer to lower the bed. When I insist she looks me straight in the eye.

"I don't like change," she says. "I'm old."

Downstairs I try to entice my mother outside into the sunshine by suggesting we take a walk to the mailbox at the end of the drive. No dice, though my mother used to love getting the mail, loved sorting the flyers and magazines and appeals for money, love hoping something good and magical had possibly come. Today I bring back only a solicitation for life insurance. My mother wants to read it but I take it gently from her hand and throw it away. Last year I went through her life insurance, discovered a dozen policies from AAA, United of Omaha, Colonial Penn. Junk policies for the most part, worth less than the amount my mother had dutifully plowed into them. Policies meant to ensnare and impoverish the vulnerable elderly. Fucking greedy predatory unregulated capitalism.

"You don't need life insurance," I tell my mother. "We're grown, all launched. You did your job."

My mother shakes her head. "You have to leave something behind," she insists. If you don't leave something behind, you've failed.

We look for something to watch on television, something to pass the hours until dinner time.

"Not Hallmark," my mother says. "I don't like Hallmark. Nothing but White people."

I laugh and tell her about all the White people I have seen on my daily walks around her neighborhood. Many, many White people, dozens upon dozens, striding the sidewalks of the upscale little neighborhood like they own them, gliding the pathway along the canal like it was made for them. Some of these White people have been genuinely friendly, like the guy who caught me jogging backward one morning and said, "You're making me feel old!" Others have been pointedly cold. I take both with all the salt in the nearby Pacific.

But on that morning's walk, for the first time, I encountered a Black woman. Seeing her lifted my spirits. She was on the other side of the street but we called out to one another over the passing traffic, hands raised in greeting, hands open to signal all was well.

"I was waving like a fool," I tell my mother, exaggerating the gesture to make her laugh.

My mother smiles. "Life is funny," she says.

"Life is funny," I echo.

My mother is eighty-five as I write this. A friend is amazed. "You're the only Black person our age I know whose parents are still alive," she says. My mother's mother died at seventy-two. I am nearing sixty. Trees can live for hundreds of years but all of us will eventually snag.

"Life is funny," my mother says again. "And then you die."

On Kindness

Last year a man I knew committed suicide. I did not know him well, mostly by sight and reputation; we said hello in the elevator, made chit chat at meetings, maybe once disagreed on some mammoth email chain. We weren't friends by a long shot. When his death became known I could not claim, like others, to be distraught. I did not wonder why (none of my business) or ask myself the question that is most tortuous for the family and friends of someone who takes their life: could I have done something to prevent it? But I did wonder about our interactions. I wondered how I had treated this person I sort of knew but had no investment in. I wondered if, in the sporadic, quotidian moments of fleeting connection between me and this other human being, I had been kind?

It's easy to answer the opposite: I was never unkind to this person. I know this to be true not only because I would remember an unkind interaction but also because I am not generally or routinely unkind. I do not mock or disparage others, don't bully or exploit. I don't shove old ladies on the subway, or tailgate on the highway, or ever, ever cut the line. I am never mean-spirited, never hostile or disrespectful or rude. Not being unkind is my default for selfish reasons: it saves time and energy and psychic wear and tear. Not being unkind is a pretty low bar on the scale of human interaction, which is why it is so surprising that so many people cannot manage it. But kindness is not just the absence of unkindness. Being nice to waiters makes me polite and not calling people names on Twitter makes me civil and smiling at people on the street makes me Southern (or, in Boston, suspect) but none of that is kindness. Kindness requires more.

Are you kind? Most people like to think so. Of the three dozen people I asked this simple question, all but one responded with a hearty and unflinching, *Yes!* Only one person said no, though a few others qualified their positive responses. (More on that later.) Most people sincerely believe themselves to be kind, and yet the world is rife with unkindness. Something is not adding up.

Am I kind? Did I, in my fleeting interactions with the colleague who killed himself, extend myself in open-hearted connection, if only for a moment? Maybe. But in truth I'm probably not nearly as kind as I like to think I am.

Probably neither are you. Though it is unkind of me to say.

～

What does it mean to be kind? I am not here interested in questions of whether or not there is such a thing as true altruism, whether people who perform acts of kindness do so because they receive some kind of emotional or psychological or social benefit from doing so. That debate seems wildly beside the point. In a world (and particularly a nation) as deeply unkind as ours it seems clear that whatever benefits accrue from enacting kindness are not nearly sufficient to outweigh the benefits of being a selfish asshole. Kindness, whatever the benefits to the giver, is still losing the race.

The *Oxford English Dictionary* defines kindness as "Having or showing a benevolent, friendly, or warm-hearted nature or disposition; ready to assist, or show consideration for, others; sympathetic, obliging, considerate." This definition helps clarify but only a little: friendliness is lovely but it is not kindness (and it is certainly not benevolence.) Consideration—being careful not to cause inconvenience or hurt to others—pushes us a little closer; if kindness is anything it is the actionable understanding that other beings matter as much as yourself. Benevolence—the disposition to do good—raises some obvious questions about goodness. The readiness to assist might be the most concrete part of the definition, and therefore the most important part.

Aristotle defined kindness as "helpfulness toward someone in need, not in return for anything, nor for the advantage of the helper himself, but for that of the person helped." This is a reasonable definition if one factors in the understanding that all human beings (and other animals) are constantly *in need* of something. Kindness operates from this understanding, extending the self across this bridge of mutual need for the sake of the other. Charity can be kind but kindness is not charity. *Charity is overrated.*

Most of the times when we think we are being kind we are simply being polite. To be polite is simply to be courteous, to behave toward other human beings with, says *Merriam-Webster*, *the appearance of* consideration, deference, tact. Thanking the waiter who brings your meal is politeness but it has nothing to do with kindness. It is possible to be exceedingly polite and also exceedingly unkind: ask members of the British Royal Family. Politeness is a good minimum requirement for human interaction, but it's only the bottom, not the top.

Nor are *niceness* or *friendliness* necessarily kindness. Last week in the grocery store the checker smiled vacantly at me as I entered his line, sang out my total in a fake cheery voice and thanked me for my purchase when we were done. He was quite pleasant but not once did he meet my eye or make a real human connection. Once he'd handed me my receipt he turned away (though there was no one else in line and I stood for a few moments struggling with the heavy bags) and as far as he was concerned I might have fallen off the earth. It's quite reasonable that niceness is all that is required in grocery store interactions but niceness is not all that is required to be truly kind.

Nor—and this is tricky—is kindness the same thing as love. If I drive my adult daughter 400 miles from Boston to Washington, DC, so that she can return to college, I am doing so because I am connected to, and invested in, her and her well-being. If my husband (who is not her father) comes along he is doing so because he is connected to me. This is called love. Love does not exist without kindness. It is not possible to misuse or abuse a person and also love them; the two actions (and love is an action, not a feeling) are diametrically opposed. But kindness is only one element of love, and is, in some ways, the easiest part. The other day, on the way to the train, I passed a disabled woman struggling toward the bank. When I asked if she needed help, she responded in Haitian, which I do not speak. In English I apologized for my lack of understanding. She gestured toward her bag, which was heavy and which she had set on the sidewalk. I picked up her bag and walked with her to the bank. The act took maybe ten minutes out of my day, cost me a little effort and care but no commitment, no knowledge, no responsibility. Kindness is a much easier lift than love. Which is why it's surprising so many of us cannot muster it. Why it makes no sense that our so-called Christian nation is, in fact, deeply, deeply unkind.

Kindness is not an American virtue. It stands uneasily alongside those values we pretend to admire—self-reliance, individualism, ambition—and directly opposite those we actually do: selfishness, dominance, greed. Americans get misty-eyed over small, individual acts of kindness on social media (especially those which are only necessary because of larger societal failures, like people banding together to buy a car for a fast food worker or cops buying shoes for a homeless vet) but disparage people committed to equity and a safety net as "social justice warriors." Our political and sports heroes, which are the only heroes we have, are often superficially pleasant, like Ronald Reagan or Tom Brady, but rarely truly kind. When they are, we mock and punish them. Ask Jimmy Carter.

In America, kindness is for suckers and everybody knows it. Nearly half of the people in my little survey qualified their declaration of kindness with some version of this: *Yes, but I worry my kindness will be exploited or abused.* Several men said they were kind but in the next breath stressed that their kindness should not be mistaken for weakness. Other men seemed to view kindness as a kind of masculine charity delivered mostly to women and kids. One man told me, "A strong man is kind to people weaker than himself."

"What about people as strong as him? Don't they need kindness?" I asked.

"Why would they?" he asked. "Anyway, being kind to other men might be misunderstood."

Kindness is prosocial behavior, but American culture is deeply anti-social. Consider this definition of antisocial personality disorder from the Mayo Clinic:

> . . . *a mental disorder in which a person consistently shows no regard for right and wrong and ignores the rights and feelings of others. Symptoms include lying or deceit to exploit others; being callous, cynical and disrespectful of*

others; arrogance, a sense of superiority and being extremely opinionated; poor or abusive relationships; repeatedly violating the rights of others through intimidation and dishonesty; lack of empathy and lack of remorse; hostility, aggression or violence.

Sound familiar? Put bluntly, our society is sociopathic. If America were a person, the kindest thing to do with us would be to get us some help.

Many belief systems, including Buddhism, posit kindness as a human instinct. So do some major schools of psychology. Even Charles Darwin believed natural selection favored the evolution of compassion. Darwin, who didn't actually coin the phrase "survival of the fittest," argued that communities of the most sympathetic individuals would flourish, raising more children than villages full of jerks, who would eventually, over time, self-extinguish.

It has taken 200 years but the United States is about to prove Mr. Darwin right.

~

Social and behavioral psychologists generally agree that personality is both genetic and environmental; we are both born and made. Kindness is like language, says psychologist Richard Davidson: most of us are born with great capacity for both. "But the expression for language requires that we be raised in a linguistic community. And similarly for kindness and compassion, we are all born with these seeds, but it requires that they be nurtured, and if they're not nurtured, they will atrophy."

Who taught me about kindness? My struggling mother received so few drops of kindness in her life she had little to pass along. Not the elite boarding school I attended on scholarship, whose motto *non sibi* no one took seriously. Not the church of my childhood, more concerned with sin and judgment than love and compassion. Not the elite college I attended or the newspapers where I began my career or the academy where I will probably end it. Not my own human heart: selfish and defensive, full of yearning and justification, full of me.

Depression taught me about kindness, depression and trying not to die. Motherhood, though motherhood itself is no magic kindness drug. Friends and partners. Reading and more reading. Love, less the finding than the wanting and the looking, which seemed endless and hurt so much and did so much damage until finally I figured out that first I must be kind to myself.

In the end all I know about kindness is that it is serious business. That, like love, kindness is something you do, not something you have or are. To become kind one must practice kindness, just as the only way to get good at pushups is to do more and then more of them. Kindness is something you plant and tend and grow, like cauliflower. Except that I've always had a hard time growing cauliflower. It's picky about growing conditions, susceptible to pests and infestation. It must be constantly watched and nurtured and tended, for fear it will be choked by weeds.

On Innocence

I'm trying to remember when I lost my innocence. By this I do not mean the first time I engaged in sexual intercourse; connecting innocence to a lack of knowledge about this single aspect of human experience has a long, complicated history in the Judeo-Christian west but not even in the Ten Commandments is it written in stone.

The innocence I mean has to do with a lack of knowledge about the world beyond one's immediate borders, fences of tribe and belief and self. This kind of innocence rests in a deep incuriosity, not the possession of illusion but the steadfast refusal to let it die. This kind of innocence is the belief that one's limited knowledge about the world is sufficient, and that any further knowledge that might be necessary will be served up warm and nicely plated, with a little parsley sprig. This kind of innocence is relentlessly and childishly self-centering. This kind of innocence is a willful blindness to the weeping elephant in the corner and the gun in one's own hands.

By this definition I lost my innocence around the age of nine or ten, when the understanding that we were Black and poor and that these things were both shameful and connected began to dawn. (The issue of internalized anti-Blackness—"Who taught you to hate yourself?"asked Malcolm—I have long since interrogated but the question of when and how impoverished people are made to carry shame is one that still interests me. Toni Morrison once remarked that the poverty of her childhood was free from stigma but the poverty of mine was coated in the stuff. Who taught you to hate yourself for being under somebody's foot?) I also came to understand that being impoverished was the source of my mother's profound stress and deep unhappiness.

This dawning awakened me to the fact that there were things I did not understand and could not explain and neither could anyone around me, at least not in a way that made sense (if Black people were poor because they were stupid and lazy why were we poor when my mother was neither of those things?) Reading helped. Books offered escape while also showing me that everybody suffered (as James Baldwin said) and that sometimes people suffered over things I had never even considered. Which meant the world must be full of such things.

The church of my childhood also helped rid me of innocence; any illusion about my own unbreachable goodness was handily dismantled every time the pastor opened his mouth. People were born wicked, an unavoidably sinful affront to God; since I was a person and as yet unsaved I was as bad as anyone. This caused some psychic distress, of course. Were I in charge I might have framed things differently, might have cast sin not as the breaking of certain (arbitrary, conflicting, power-reinforcing) rules but the intentional or unintentional wounding of other beings, of the world and of myself. Still, in the end it was a useful lesson: by the time I was eleven or twelve I understood I was as capable as anybody of being rotten enough to make Jesus cry.

The shedding of this kind of innocence is not a loss, but a necessity for any person who wants to be not only an adult but a moral one. "People who shut their eyes to reality simply invite their own destruction, and anyone who insists on remaining in a state of innocence long after that innocence is dead turns himself into a monster," wrote Baldwin, who certainly knew about monsters. But leaving this state of innocence behind is challenging in a country where innocence is willfully, steadfastly, determinedly maintained, a country which expends a great deal of time and energy on shutting its eyes not only to the world but to its own history. In America distraction is abundant, self-questioning discouraged, shutting one's eyes to reality the national sport. In America optimism is the greatest possible virtue, far superior to intelligent wrestling. It was Obama's sunny optimism which won him the presidency, not his intellect. Americans liked the vision of racial harmony he both represented and insisted was possible, without, notably, either sacrifice or pain.

Watching the movie *Elf* one Christmas I began thinking about all the movies in which the protagonist is, essentially, a child in an adult body, an overgrown innocent. *Forrest Gump,*

Big, Being There, Bill and Ted, The 40-Year-Old-Virgin and all those other Judd Apatow movies (I assume, not having actually watched them), and most movies starring Will Farrell or Adam Sandler or certain other comedians from *Saturday Night Live* (I haven't watched these either, so this is a guess.) As with the bulk of angry/drunk/disgruntled heroes in redemption movies (*The Wrestler, The Master, Gran Torino, Crazy Heart*) innocent heroes seem to be mostly male. Rare is the *contemporary* (hat tip to Audrey Hepburn and Doris Day) movie with a naive innocent female protagonist; when there is, she's usually a princess (*Enchanted, The Princess Diaries, The Princess Bride*) or a robot (*Her, Cherry 2000, The Stepford Wives*), making the story either a fairytale or a male fantasy. In the rare instances where a real live human adult woman is the lead innocent, things tend to be harder for her rather than easier (*Nell*) or she has to lose the innocence to get the man (Sandy in *Grease.*) As for innocent Black lead characters, especially Black women . . . well, dear reader, I will leave the compilation of that list to you. It shouldn't take very long. In America, Black people are not allowed to be innocent, not even on film. Unless they're Morgan Freeman and/or dead.

Once upon a time I spoke at a retirement village not far from my town. This manufactured village of elegant, one-story villas and well-appointed apartments surrounded by pine-studded hills and tennis courts was home to kind and well-meaning people, educated and curious, the youngest in their sixties, the oldest well beyond. They were also, all of them, White, at least as far as I could tell.

What struck me most about the crowd was their ageless innocence. They were completely unfamiliar, for example, with the concept of internalized racism, of the damage inflicted on the self-esteem of Black children by White supremacy. Only a few were familiar with the famous doll tests conducted by Dr. Kenneth Clark and cited as part of his testimony during *Brown v Board of Education* in 1954. They were shocked when I said the first place I was called nigger was not my hometown of Memphis but New Hampshire—and disbelieving when I said that of all the places I have lived, north and south, Boston was the most segregated. That anyone should profess *surprise* at Boston's segregation is astonishing; not only is the fact frequently reported, it is glaringly self-evident. All you have to do is drive around and look.

This visit took place during the middle years of the Reign of Trump, long after the shock should have passed. I would not hazard to guess the political affiliation of the good people of the retirement village in general but the group which came out to see me were, for the most part, opposed to Trump and his anti-Black, anti-immigrant, anti-democratic and otherwise anti-social ways. How in the world, they wanted to know, had America elected such a person? This was not the country they knew, the country they loved. Except, of course, it was. And is.

One well-intentioned woman held up a copy of Robin DeAngelo's *White Fragility* and said it made her "feel terrible," thereby not so much missing the point as trampling obliviously over it. Another woman—I swear to you—asked if I knew why no Black couples had moved into their little community since the "two we had" died. A third woman asked if the fact that we were now, in her words, "inundated" with commercials featuring interracial couples and biracial children did not signal major progress. I should have asked, "Major progress in what?" because that is the operative question, but I was too taken aback. This was the first time I'd heard this argument, though it would not be the last. Setting aside the question of whether an increase from zero to some equals inundation, a belief that decreasing White disapproval of interracial marriage (for it is White disapproval we mean here; Black people have always largely "approved" of such relationships) as represented by commercials means significant progress in the dismantling of structural racial inequity in everything from the criminal justice system to school discipline to mortgage lending to house appraisals to health care policy to residential pollution (supporting evidence for all this in the works cited page at the end of the book or you might, dear reader, take the initiative and look it up) to a thousand other areas is simply ludicrous, and based on the misguided belief that racism is about "feelings" instead of power. It is these feelings that allow White people to believe we have made great progress in racial equality. Reparations? Nope. Structural change? No, thank you. A full and truthful reckoning of American history taught to American children? Don't make me laugh. But I won't call out the hounds if you marry my neighbor's sister. Maybe I'll even let you marry my own.

The well-intentioned woman who felt "terrible" also proudly informed us that she had been going to Antiqua for thirty years and had formed a loving relationship with the people there, people she considered family. This single data point proved that happy "race relations" (a misdirectional phrase meant not to illuminate but to conceal if ever one existed) were possible.

"If they could figure it out in Antiqua," she asked, "why can't we?"

Where to even begin? One place was to say that of course I could not speak to this woman's *particular* experience with her "Antiquan family" (it would have been cruel for me to ask if she routinely brought them presents or otherwise supported them financially or to point out that White perceptions of "race relations" are not always to be trusted, that all throughout American history White people have sworn themselves to be "just like family" with Black people who considered them anything but, that a White woman used to say the same thing about my great aunt who worked for her for twenty years and hated the woman's guts) but that this one bit of connection said zilch about existing power structures in Antigua, let alone the United States. Did she know the political situation in Antigua? Did she know the nation's history?

"No," she admitted. "Well, a little. They weren't slaves."

Having never been to Antigua and knowing nothing about

its history, I nevertheless assured her the ancestors of the people of African descent living on that fertile Caribbean island were almost certainly enslaved. How in the world did she think they got there in the first place? Wrong turn in the North Atlantic? A doomed three-hour tour?

I want to be careful here. My intent is neither to chastise nor to mock. It's not even, really, to express surprise. Any Black person in America who speaks and writes or even just thinks about White supremacy and structural racism is well-acquainted with this kind of wide-eyed defiance of our collective racial reality. I laughed out loud at reading stories in *The Washington Post* about White people complaining about having to hear about slavery while touring Southern plantations. That same resistance to history often dogs White students who take my African American literature classes and complain about having to learn about slavery (slave narratives) or Black resistance (*David Walker's Appeal*) or Red Summer ("If We Must Die") or northern racism (*Native Son)* and on and on. My teaching evaluations often praise my knowledge, passion and dedication but ask why I can't lighten things up a little? "My only thing I do warn people about is the fact that the class is highly pessimistic," wrote one student on Rate My Professor. "If you're looking for a fun class, this is not it."

Hahahaha.

My intent is neither to chastize nor to mock but just, I guess, to wonder what living inside such innocence feels like.

It must be comforting. Even the words we use—the words I'm using—to describe this phenomenon of Whiteness are soft and squishy: *innocence, fragility*. Even the shaking words are meant to cushion. Even the wake-up call is a lullaby.

～

At that retirement village, one of the good people asked me about the future, asked if I did not believe that things were getting better in America. This is a common occurrence; White people are forever asking me—demanding, really—to predict, for this county they love, a future magically free of inequality, injustice and White supremacy. This good person at the retirement village asked if I was hopeful that things would get better and back on track once we "got rid of all these racists."

"When will that be?" I should have asked. Instead, both frustrated and bored, I responded with a long, rambling story about first traveling abroad when I was nineteen and returning through JFK Airport and having the passport control agent say "Welcome home" and bursting into tears because, for the first time, I felt truly American. It's precisely because I am truly American that, although I believe this nation *could* change and grow and eventually live up to its myth of itself, I do not believe it ever will. By "all these racists," the good person in the retirement village meant only Trump and his sycophants. But Trump was the symptom not the disease; neither Trump nor the circle of racists who surrounded and enabled him nor even the ones who voted angrily to put him into office make me hold this opinion. The good people in the retirement village are the primary reason I believe this country will never change.

It's not the malevolence that makes me unhopeful. It's the innocence.

On Throwing a Party

On the day of the party I tell myself I will never, ever do this again.

By mid-morning I have been up and prepping since dawn. There is much to be done, beginning with all the baking and cooking. Already a pumpkin cheesecake intensifies in the fridge and a poolish for the bread bubbles in the cooler but that's just the start of it. Rule #1 of throwing a party is that the worst possible outcome is somebody leaving hungry. The first time I took my White husband-to-be home to meet my Black, southern mother she set out both a turkey and a ham, plus all the fixins, and there were centuries in that offering. Centuries.

As an adolescent I cooked because I had to; my mother rightfully figured one benefit of raising five children alone had to be offloading some of the chores. Out on my own after college I subsisted mostly on pasta and salads and sandwiches, not because I could not cook (see above) but because I didn't care. When my children came along I understood quite clearly from the Mommy blogs and the Mommy mags and the Mommy shows and the pediatrician and the Olympic-level mommies at my children's schools that my job was to provide food that was healthy, nutritious, organic, palate-expanding and delightful to the eye at Every Single Meal. Even then I knew it was, at best, churlish, in a world of starving people, to complain about the drudgery of putting three meals a day on the table when the hardest thing I had to manage was taking toddlers through the cereal aisle, I tried not to complain. I learned to cook and tolerate it, and to bake and love it and to take satisfaction in nurturing my children. Still, by the time my son reached high school I was pretty much done. When they left home I ate salads and sandwiches and cereal. Except at party time.

Party cooking is pleasure cooking. Party cooking is earnest but short-term effort, with maximum reward. Party cooking is a chance to nurture in containment, a chance to delight in making vegan for the vegans and vegetarian for the vegetarians and homemade bread for everybody and chocolate pumpkin cheesecake for those who cannot help themselves. Party cooking is a chance to show off and show out and experiment with dishes that are too complex or cumbersome or time-consuming to prepare for one or two. And when the party's over your fridge will overflow with leftovers, both the stuff you make and the stuff that other people brought, and you will not have to cook until Thursday, if you work it right.

❧

By noon I am cleaning. For a Black woman from Memphis the second worst possible outcome when people come to your house is that somebody notices dirt. Or the bathroom has odors or the dog hair tumbles in the corner or the refrigerator smells. I am an adequate housekeeper, maintaining an acceptable level of cleanliness and orderliness for my own sanity. But party cleaning is like spring cleaning. Put away are the sneakers you've been stepping around all winter. Thrown away are the dead flowers and stacked newspapers and crumbled gum wrappers you have long ceased to see. The floors are not just swept but mopped, the door handles and light fixtures disinfected, the walls wiped down, the windowsills cleaned. Even after twelve or twenty people have tramped through, my house will be cleaner after the party than it was in the days before. A clean, orderly house is pleasurable. It's like falling in love with your house all over again.

Around two in the afternoon the phone calls begin. Rule #2 of throwing a party is to never answer the phone on party day. Nobody is lost (GPS,) nobody has questions: the only people calling on party day are calling to blow you off. On party day, blow-offs are irrelevant. The train has left the station and it will either reach its destination or crash. The only thing party-day cancellations can accomplish is to intensify the already-creeping fear that your party will be a disaster, everyone will be miserable and you will never be able to show your face again.

To throw a party is to make oneself vulnerable. A party is an emery board against the ego, shaping as it files. This, more than the hassle or the expense, is the reason many people never host. An invitation to one's home is an invitation to one's most intimate space, and, like any invitation, it risks rejection. Or acceptance and subsequent disappointment, which is always worse. The worst party I ever threw happened on New Year's Eve. Rule #3 of throwing a party: never throw a party on New Year's Eve. I had the bright idea to invite every single man I knew and to have my single girlfriends do the same, a kind of swap meet of good-guy-but-not-right-for-me potential partners. The men did their part, dutifully arriving with warm hopes and chilled prosecco but for some reason all but one girlfriend stayed home, creating a male-to-female ratio of something like ten to one. It made for an awkward evening. After that disaster I swore I would never have another party. And yet I have and I do and I will, maybe. Probably. Yes.

⌒

Every party is a failure in its first hour. Some people have arrived precisely on time (don't do this) and stand around awkwardly not talking and watching you take the last of the food out of the oven. The lights are still too bright and for some reason your Bose has decided to be temperamental. You wonder about those phone calls: how many are not coming? You wonder about the food: will people like it? You wonder about the evening, now stretching endlessly out before you: will the people who made such an effort to be there enjoy themselves, or simply endure it? Will everyone who shows up have a good time?

This first hour—when the guests trickle in and the conversation stalls and the scent of failure hangs like Lemon Pledge in the air—is the hour of regret. What could have been a quiet evening at home is now become a burden, a responsibility to entertain and be entertained. I become exhausted and cranky and inclined toward hunkering down. So does everyone else. I can see that, see right through their bright party clothes to the tiredness and weathering inside. We are, all of us, exhausted. This is an exhausting country in which to live. The inclination runs toward withdrawal, hides in retreat. Every person for herself in such dangerous times.

But we stand around and make bright chatter and I lower the lights and then suddenly somebody laughs, really laughs. Then somebody listens, really listens. In the living room two people sit on the couch in conversation, revealing themselves. By the second hour of the party I have turned it all over to the spirit: whatever happens is no longer in my hands. Everyone who is coming has arrived. The wine is flowing, the music playing, the food being happily devoured. Everywhere I look are people I know and cherish, people from all walks of my life gathered together under one roof, talking and laughing, connecting face-to-face. Whether the party is large or small, a dance party for my fiftieth birthday or a small dinner party in honor of friends, something important is happening, something that extends far beyond me and even beyond the people invited. Something bigger. Something necessary.

Like many people, I am deeply skeptical of contemporary calls for civility. Such calls are usually meant to silence those crying out against injustice, oppression and discrimination, all of which are very uncivil things. I am, however, in favor of calls for more community. Community is deeply lacking in the United States; like our savage form of capitalism, our cult of individualism has long ago become monstrous, metastasizing into a cancer of selfishness. Toni Morrison once pointed out how even the words used by politicians and marketers have pushed this progression toward me-ism: "When I was a young girl we were called citizens—American citizens. We were second-class citizens, but that was the word. In the fifties and sixties they started calling us consumers. So we did—consume. Now they don't use those words any more—it's the American taxpayer and those are different attitudes."

Throwing a party for my friends and neighbors will not solve this problem. But throwing a party is not only an antidote to my own selfishness, it is a small way to nurture the collective, to battle the tendency, even among people who tend to vote the same way or hold the same values, to stay at home during times of turmoil. Throwing a party is my way of reminding the people in my circles that we are in this thing together, and that even in the midst of crisis, there is room for simple, human joy.

The best party I ever threw was a few years ago, one put

together for no particular reason except to welcome fall. On a whim, I asked several people to bring instruments—guitars and fiddle and even the bagpipes. I dug up every tamborine and maraca and djembe I could find in my house, which turned out, to my surprise, to be a lot. When the playing and singing started, some people were skeptical at first, held back by their weekday selves, their masks and personas, their boundaries and authorities. But after a while all of that melted. Everyone joined in, if only by clapping their hands.

~

Somebody turns up the music and we begin to dance. And the spirit descends and the party becomes a gathering and the gathering becomes community. We dance together and sing together and laugh together like there is no place else on earth we'd rather be than there, together.

I let go of the party and the party catches us all.

On Learning to Ride a Motorcycle
After Fifty and Other Pursuits

For one thing, it was raining: a chilly, damp October morning much better spent having coffee in my living room.

For another thing we got yelled at. We arrived ten minutes late, frantic and rushing because I had stalled getting out of the house (see first paragraph) and because our GPS took us mistakenly to a Dunkin Donuts instead of the motorcycle shop where we were supposed to be. The instructor stopped the class to berate us, complaining that he would now have to go over all the things he had already gone over, which turned out mostly to be a warning against being late and also the locations of the bathrooms. The chastisement was deserved but also kind of ridiculous; the instructor puffed and pouted as though our lateness was a personal affront, as if we'd been late just to ruin his day. (I'm a teacher; students show up late, it happens.) Had he acted with more grace I would have gone to him during the break and apologized, would have taken responsibility for finding out what we missed from a classmate, would have volunteered to skip a break or stay after to learn where the bathrooms were. Instead I soured immediately, not only on him, but on the entire experience. The class was fifteen minutes old and I hated everything about it. I hadn't even sat on the bike yet.

My husband loves motorcycles. He bought his first bike at sixteen, to the dismay and bewilderment of his parents. He rode into his twenties and into his first marriage, until children came along and he gave it up as being too dangerous. For twenty years he maintained his license, dutifully renewing it with the idea that he would climb back aboard a bike when his children no longer depended upon him. Two months after his youngest daughter left for college he cleaned out the garage, bought a bike and began taking it out on weekends, then on overnight trips and then on weeklong adventures to foreign lands.

When I ask my husband what he loves about motorcycles, he speaks about the wind on his face, being flooded by the smell of grass and earth and rain, the feeling of hurtling down the road with nothing between him and the elements. It is also, he admits, the danger, the knowing that a careless moment or unskilled action could lead to tragedy. It is, he says, about the conquering of fear, and about autonomy, about being alone on his bike with no one to answer to, or to depend on, except himself. (This is all very interesting, but does not quite, I think, explain why every middle-aged man I know owns either a motorcycle, a truck, a boat, a fancy pedal bike costing more than my (used) car or a collection of expensive musical instruments—or all of the above. I think there's something else.)

Motorcycles have never interested me. I like the wind and the smell of grass as much as anyone but have no interest in courting danger and no desire to face any more fears than absolutely necessary. Before the class I'd only been on precisely two bikes. The first one belonged to an ex-boyfriend I was hoping would become my boyfriend again. I was seventeen and on break from school and went to New York and he took me for a spin around Manhattan that was equal parts terrifying and exhilarating. The boy did not become my boyfriend again but at least I had a story to tell. The second time was shortly after my husband got his BMW. Our spin around the neighborhood lasted less than ten minutes and felt exactly like being the helpless passenger on the back of someone's pedal bike, only faster and thus more dangerous. I hated it.

But I wouldn't hate it if I were the one *in control* of the motorcycle, my husband suggested. Wasn't I curious? Didn't I want to learn? Riding a motorcycle was a skill like any other, like knowing how to change a tire or make a fire or handle simple home repairs. Useful to know. Especially when the apocalypse comes and the roads are gridlocked with frightened people in cars trying to flee the danger.

"Only bikes will be able to get through."

This was back in 2018 and 2019, when we joked often about the coming apocalypse, by which we meant not an unforeseen pandemic or a nightmarish eruption of zombies but the entirely predictable and inevitable breakdown of American society, spurred by an uprising of aggrieved White supremacists and other cultists and resulting eventually in an outbreak of civil war. Meaning, we weren't really joking at all.

Which is why one day, in response to my husband's lighthearted insistence that I needed to be able to climb aboard his motorcycle and flee if the apocalypse happened while he was away from home, I laughed and said, "Yeah. I guess it would be good to take a class."

Five weeks later I stood in a cold October rain being scolded by a guy whose helmet covered only half his face and looked like a costume from *Hogan's Heroes*. I hated the rain, hated the cold, hated that guy.

But none of these were the reason I hated the motorcycle class.

～

I am good at many things. I can grow vegetables, bake from scratch, cook for a family—or a dinner party, as we have seen—without embarrassing myself. I can read maps and navigate foreign cities and make minor household repairs. I can do a headstand and paint a room and tile a backsplash and operate a jackhammer. I'm an excellent driver, a fine teacher and a compelling public speaker. I can carry a tune and not embarrass myself on the dance floor. I can take direction, decipher texts and get out splinters. I'm a competent writer; I know how to get my point across.

I am good at many things, but, of course, it is possible I overestimate my abilities, à la the Dunning-Kruger Effect. It's possible I think myself more capable than I am precisely because I lack the skills to accurately self-evaluate.

But I think it is more likely that I am objectively competent at the limited number of activities in which I engage not only because I've been doing them so long, but also because being competent is *the reason* I do them in the first place. Maybe even things I've learned later in life—like how to tile a backsplash or teach an online class or supervise other human beings—simply built upon what were already baseline competencies. Maybe I've kept learning and being successful at learning mostly because the growth has come in areas that already played to my strengths. Maybe everything new I've learned since I was young has played straight to my strengths.

For the first part of our lives, we learn unconsciously, at a breathtaking pace. By the age of ten I had learned at least a thousand things I did know at birth: how to walk and talk and eat with utensils, how to dress myself and tie my shoes and brush my teeth, how to read and write and listen, how to obey and also how to resist.

But at some point, learning becomes conscious. When that happens, to continue learning we must believe we *need t*o learn, must feel ourselves lacking in some area, absent some skill or piece of knowledge which holds the potential to improve our life. This comes easily to children, who are told in constant word and deed that their primary job is to acquire the accumulated knowledge presumably held by members of the adult world. But the older we get the more difficult it is to see, and to acknowledge, our inadequacies.

When my son was contemplating a year abroad in high school, we went to an informational meeting for the program he would attend. An alumnus of the program, a sweet-faced young man, was asked how hard it was to immerse oneself in a language you did not understand. "Not hard at all," the young man said, "you just have to be willing to constantly look like an idiot."

Learning is hard on the ego. Despite teaching for decades— or perhaps because of teaching for decades—I'd forgotten that.

It would certainly explain why I hated the motorcycle class.

~

The basic rider course, approved by the Commonwealth of Massachusetts, requires four hours of classroom learning and ten hours of on-cycle training over two days. There are twelve of us in the class, including myself and my husband, who takes the class as moral support and also because he loves motorcycles. See above.

Leading us on this adventure are Sam The Scolder and another instructor named Zeke. Sam we suspect, from his authoritarian posturing and doughy body, of being a cop, but Zeke is shorter, more muscled and also far more chill. Less

CHIPS, more Zen.

The course is scheduled to run all day Saturday and Sunday and conclude with written and skills tests. If I pass both, I'll be allowed to stop in the motorcycle store on the way out and legally drive home a machine capable of reaching 200 miles per hour and thirty-seven times more likely than an automobile to result in my death. Like many things in America, this is insane, but never mind.

Because it is raining, the class begins indoors, inside a massive warehouse stocked with Harleys and Ducatis and Indians (ugh on the name, ugh on the bike) and ATVs and snowmobiles and other expensive toys. We choose our bikes— everyone else has already chosen theirs, the instructor points out—and spend the first thirty or so minutes getting familiar with the controls: here's the throttle, here's the clutch, here's the brake. I make special note of the brake. We spend an eternity discussing when to use the choke. The answer, my husband will tell me later, is never, since most modern bikes don't have one.

My Honda Nighthawk 250s is a good thirty years old and bears the scars of many a drop. Besides injury, dropping the bike is my biggest worry, one which intensifies when I realize I'm the only woman in the class. Dropping the bike gets you serious demerits. I am not going to be the Girl Who Dropped the Bike.

I am also the only Black person, though the class is otherwise diverse, surprisingly so. One guy's from Russia, another from Italy; both are college students, which makes sense. There's a man from India and another from somewhere in Central America. He is, he tells us, recently married. ("When I told my wife I wanted a motorcycle, she burst into tears.")

The remaining students are, like my husband, White. One, a tall, neat, good-looking young man in his early thirties, listens to the introductions then says, in a voice straight out of *The Departed*, "Lotta accents in this class."

"Yep," I say. "Including yours."

He stares at me a moment, then laughs. His name is Riley. Unlike Sam, he turns out to be a cop.

The youngest student is seventeen. Only three of us, including me and my husband, are old enough to remember a time before the internet or ovens that microwave. Being an elder or whatever we're called and learning to ride a motorcycle is strange and not a little embarrassing, like showing up, dressed and grinning, at a BTKS concert, or crashing a prom.

Outside in the drizzle we start the bikes, fiddle around some more with the controls and then, astonishingly, begin to ride. The routine for the class is quickly established: Sam outlines a drill, Zeke demonstrates, we line up and try it ourselves, failing or succeeding in plain view. We practice basic skills—starting and stopping, shifting and stopping, using the clutch and finding the friction zone. Though I've driven a standard shift car for years, the friction zone on the bike eludes me, raising my frustration, which, in turn, makes my performance worse. Every drill I feel more like Chevy Chase playing Gerald Ford (you have to be a certain age to get the reference.) I drive too slow, stop too soon, go the wrong way around the marker. Finding neutral feels impossible; over and over I shift through and stall. Part of the problem is that the bike is too small and my boots, dug out of the closet and borrowed from one of my kids, too clunky and big, but in the moment I don't make this connection. In the moment I feel incompetent.

The afternoon is easier. Sam departs, off to scold jaywalkers and people who leave leaves on their lawns. We retreat inside, to a cluttered classroom that smells faintly of stale fast food but at least is warm and dry. It's Zeke's turn to lead; his instruction method involves having us read portions of the textbook aloud then pausing to discuss. This is not innovative teaching but it gets the job done, the job being cramming enough information into our heads for us to pass the written test. When it's my turn I read fluidly and answer questions with a snap. In a classroom I am hyper-competent. In a classroom, I am home.

The motorcycle textbook focuses mostly on ways to stay safe while riding: dress appropriately, remain visible, anticipate rather than react to the actions of others. Always have an escape path, or two. Know your risk offset and operate within it. Risk offset, explains Zeke, is the difference between the risks you take and the skills you possess. Low risk, high skills is the gold standard. High risk, high skills, okay. Low risk, low skills is reasonable, especially to begin. The person most likely to get into trouble riding a motorcycle is the person who takes high risks with a low skill set, risking their life on abilities insufficient to the task at hand.

Risk offset. The concept almost makes the entire grumpy day worthwhile.

Zeke is a gentle teacher, gentle in the way of men who have nothing to prove. He's a veteran ("I got back on the bike when I came back from Afghanistan. My wife couldn't say no,") loving father (his daughter keeps calling because their guinea pig died) and country boy who's taken his share of spills and learned that what mattered on the road was not speed or noise or badassery or any other kind of macho cosplay. What matters is enjoying the ride and coming home. "You may be right: that guy who cut you off may be an asshole," Zeke says. "The question is: do you want to be right, or do you want to be alive?"

This reminds me of a question a therapist once asked me, one that changed my life. *Do you want to be right, or do you want to be loved?*

In class, everyone nods their heads as Zeke raises his eyebrows. The right answer to his question is obvious. But the honest answer, the answer I gave the therapist, the answer no one speaks aloud, is: *Both.*

～

Day Two we arrive twenty minutes early, bearing boxes of donuts and hot coffee to ward off the morning chill. The donuts are my husband's idea: there is no quicker way to win friends and influence people than to offer deep-fried food. Later, as we drive the college students back to their train, they will tell us how Sam, who picked them up from the station that morning, spent the commute trashing us and wondering if we'd be late again. Instead, we stand and watch Sam hustle to finish setting up the course as the arriving students gleefully stuff their faces. When Sam sheepishly asks for a donut, my husband winks.

Day Two focuses on control of the bike: S-turns and U-turns and maneuvering. Also on tap are ways to get out of trouble on the road. As in life, Zeke tells us, the question is not whether trouble will come, but when. On a motorcycle, trouble comes often in the form of sudden obstacles. You're riding down the road and a deer leaps from the bushes, or the school bus in front of you suddenly breaks or a board falls from the back of a truck. The choice, when faced with a sudden obstacle, is to either swerve, ride over or try to stop, and this is a choice best made ahead of time. Zeke gives us a scenario: you're riding down a beautiful country lane when suddenly a ball rolls out of a driveway, followed, for all you know, by a child. What do you?

"Stop," I say.

"That's a lot of people's instinct," Zeke says. "But that instinct is usually wrong." When trouble comes in the form of a sudden obstacle you probably won't have time to stop. Even if you do, the guy right behind you may not. The right choice, in this case, Zeke says, is probably to swerve into your escape lane, the one you've previously identified. The one you've kept at the back of your mind. Always have an escape lane.

We practice racing across the parking lot (racing being a relative term) and then swerving around a barrier, first to the right, then to the left, then to whichever side Zeke points at the last minute. We practice riding over boards and cutting tight corners. We practice riding fast down a long strip and coming to a hard stop on a line without losing the bike. The young men love it. They chatter happily as they wait their turn to perform, revving their motors to hear the sound. The one other older man smiles quietly, keeping mostly to himself. My husband, the star of the class, leads each exercise at the request of the instructors, too tall for his tiny bike but enjoying himself. Everybody but me is having a good time.

"Does she ever smile?" Sam asks my husband, though not in my hearing. Sam is an asshole but not an idiot.

After two hours of maneuvers, it's time for the road test. My heart thumps and my palms, beneath the thin leather gloves I am wearing, sweat. Even in the moment I know this is ridiculous. I have no plans to actually get a motorcycle, no plans to take long rides on a summer day the way my husband does. If I fail the test, if I don't get the license, my life will not change. Moreover, my husband told me the last time he took the course (at another school), everyone in the class passed, including a woman who crashed her bike. These guys are in the business of putting people on the road, not keeping them off. I'm not even the worst person in the class; that would be a young, lanky guy wearing dress shoes and drugstore knit gloves who comes oh-so-close to dropping his bike. If I don't pass the test it doesn't matter one whit. Still, I want to do well, not for the people who I will never see again, not even for my husband, but for myself. Learning may slow as we age but the ego never relents.

I don't do well. My turns go outside the lines and my swerves take me right into the back of the imaginary bus. I accelerate too slowly and brake far too soon and my feet touch the ground while I'm turning a slow figure eight. Even as I'm still testing I know that my performance is inadequate. There are only a certain number of points you can lose and it is certain that I have lost those points. I know that I have failed.

"Pass," says Zeke. To everyone. The college students grin.

I pull Zeke aside as the others hustle toward the classroom to take the written test. I don't know it yet, but I will not only achieve a perfect score on the written assessment, but will find myself racing to finish first, to leap up mere minutes after the test begins and hand the paper to Zeke with a flourish of victory—scoring a perfect one hundred.

I didn't pass, I insist. It doesn't matter if I wasn't the worst one in the class. It doesn't matter if I was close enough. I don't want a mercy D, I want the F I earned. I didn't pass and I want him to say as much. I am not, it turns out, the kind of person who is good at *everything* she does. Only a person fairly good at acknowledging reality.

PART THREE

Goodbye to All That

Stella

The day after my dog died I had to go away for a weekend wedding. This was a good and joyful thing, both in its own right and for the distraction it provided. For three days I focused on traveling and rehearsal dinners and supporting my husband and celebrating his daughter and her fiance and meeting strangers and getting safely home again. I was proud of how well I was handling my dog's passing but you know what they say about pride and falling. I can see now that I am not going to get out of grief. Or guilt. I am strangely wracked with guilt, wondering if I did the right thing at the right moment and for the right reasons. This morning I woke up thinking, *My God. I killed my dog.*

Stella was old. Stella is gone. Let me tell you about Stella.

One thing, though: this is not a story about how my dog taught me to love or live or be a better human being. Dogs are easy to love, which is why people love them, but human learning seldom comes from ease. Anything important, anything lasting or worthwhile, I've learned has come only through great effort. Sometimes discomfort. Not infrequently pain. Dogs may teach us how to love other animals but not how to love other human beings, which is by far the harder job. As for teaching us how to *be* loved, unconditionally and uncritically, with devotion that borders on submission and adoration that borders on worship— well, that always seemed to me a set-up. I wasn't falling for that.

If dogs made us better people, the United States, with our 70 million dogs and the $90 billion we spend on their (and our other pets') care, would be the kindest, fairest, most loving and most humane country on Earth. Spoiler alert: we aren't.

Dogs do have something to teach us about life, about living in the moment and treating every walk around the block with the fresh joy of discovery. Dogs may even have something to teach us about aging and death, but most of us are too distracted or otherwise determined not to listen. I know I was.

❧

Stella was a stray when she came to us. Someone found her gallivanting through the streets of Boston and took her to the local animal shelter, where we encountered her. My children were reeling from the death of their beloved Lucy, a dog present in their lives from the day they were born. More keenly they mourned the destruction of their family; their father and I had just divorced. I could not replace the family but I could replace the dog and felt I had to do so. Even though I didn't want to.

I like animals but I am not sentimental about them. The dogs we had when I was growing up in Memphis lived in a mudroom on the side of the house. We fed them and played with them and loved them but they were pets, not members of the family. They never slept on our beds or climbed all over the sofa or even came into the house. (My mother spent her formative years on her grandfather's Mississippi farm where animals were largely utilitarian, treated with dignity but not like human beings.) Our two dogs, Weepie and Mr. Carter, ate mostly scraps, slept on old blankets, and never, that I recall, went to the vet. At some point they left us though I do not remember when or why. If I had to guess I would say they became too much for a woman struggling mightily to raise five Black children on her own.

When Lucy died I had no desire for another animal. I was raising half as many children as my mother (technically less than half) and, with far greater help and resources, I still felt overwhelmed with the demands: physical, financial, emotional. Why add to the burden? Dogs are great but dogs are also a great deal of work and a great deal of commitment and they depend on you so much. Too much.

But: the children. I gave in. We began the search, visiting the shelters around Boston every weekend, scanning the rescue organizations online. Buying from a breeder was out; even if I had $1,000 to spend on a dog, which I did not, I would never do so. I tried the breed-specific rescue organizations and was shocked at the requirements, at the level of scrutiny: We need your blood type and the last names of all your friends. Is your yard fenced? Will the dog have its own room? Will you commit to walking him six hours a day?

America.

It was sheer luck that brought us Stella. She had just arrived at the animal shelter, was not yet officially up for adoption and so not "on display." But one of the attendants, a beautiful Black man with locs, warned us away from another dog with, he said, a hidden aggressive streak and introduced us instead to this bright-eyed, silky-haired bundle of fur. My daughter fell in love. "Come back in seven days," the attendant said. "If no one claims her, she's yours."

In many ways she was perfect. Young but not a puppy, already housebroken, a healthy, medium-sized mutt. I am not a person who understands the appeal of little dogs. If I'm going to the trouble of a canine I want one who resembles, in size and action, the wolf from which it came. Stella was big enough to keep strangers at a respectful distance, to emit a bark that backed door-to-door salesmen down the stairs. She was striking, marked like a cross between a Bernese Mountain Dog and a black lab. Not all dogs are beautiful, but Stella was.

She was not, however, the sharpest knife in the drawer, or so I thought. In the early days, when she frustrated me with her goofy, inexhaustible energy, her chewing of vacuum cords and random slippers, her constant following me through the house, I called her my dumb blonde (sorry.) We were kicked out of obedience class when she would not focus, distracting the other dogs by approaching their owners. I clicked that little clicker a million times but never really trained her. She would sit (after a few reminders) and maybe, maybe lie down, but only until she forgot what she was supposed to be doing. She never stayed; if you left the room, she was leaving with you.

Outside she was an escape artist, slipping her lead or breaking her unbreakable line to head off on a walkabout. I liked to say we named her Stella because she was always running away. *Stella! Stella!* Once she ran through someone's open door and right onto their kitchen, startling the woman at the sink. Another time she took off after a deer as we were walking in the Blue Hills, gleefully ignoring my panicked calls. Three hours later someone found her on the other side of the reservation, miles from where I'd lost her. They took her to the Milton Animal League, where by that time she was known to the volunteers. *Stella is here again. Bring your checkbook for the fine.* That dog cost me a lot of money.

But the children loved her. She let them brush her and ride her and pull her tail and never put her mouth on them, not even once, not even if they accidentally got too rough. She slept in my daughter's room, easing her nighttime fears, and stood guard if I had to work late or run to the store. She was love for them in the midst of their post-divorce grieving. She filled in the gaps.

❧

Children grow up, if one is lucky. My daughter and son went off to school, leaving Stella for me to care for. Leaving both of us behind.

A dog is a presence in the house another being, another beating heart. This is a comfort beyond words, beyond articulate thought. We are social animals, even those of us who shrink from the crowd, who revel in solitude. We are social animals, our existence affirmed in the presence and acknowledgement of other sentient beings. Stella was always somewhere in the house but usually she was with me, sprawled in the middle of the kitchen floor as I cooked, curled up on the rug in my office as I wrote, trotting along as I moved from bedroom to dining room to side porch. When I went outside to mow the lawn or check the garden, she went too. When I went upstairs to take a shower she came along, unless, as in her final days when the arthritis was bad, I blocked the stairs, in which case she sat at the bottom and barked, affronted. Didn't I know her job was to be ever under foot?

A dog is another presence in the house and thus also an obligation, sometimes a weight. Children grow more and more independent; your job is to help that process, to work for the day when your presence is not needed, when your parenting becomes unnecessary, even irrelevant. Dogs remain ever dependent, not because they cannot care for themselves but because we've structured the relationship otherwise. When my children left home people warned me about the coming empty nest loneliness. Their warnings were well-intentioned but unnecessary; as long as I knew my children were happy and well I was perfectly content to live daily life without them, and often not a little relieved. I cooked when I wanted, ate what I wanted, left the house clean with the certainty it would be just as clean upon reentry. I came and went as I pleased whenever I pleased without worry about its impact on anyone else . . . except the dog. The dog still needed me to be home for dinner, to rise early enough to let her out. The dog still needed me to go to the store for food even if I was happy to eat only cereal until the cereal ran out. The dog still needed me and that was okay but also a little tiring after years of being the person that two other beings needed the most. For people who need to be needed, the perpetual dependence of pets is part of the appeal. For me, Stella's dependence was not a feature but a bug.

There's a woman in my neighborhood, a woman with a small brown dog of some kind, maybe a Terrier. Every day she passes my house deep in conversation with her animal, a loud and consistent running stream of inquiry and explanation: *Shall we do another block? Are you smelling the grass? That's an acorn. It turns into an oak tree if we bury it. And that's a mushroom, don't eat that it might be poisonous. I know you're hungry. When we get home we can drive to the supermarket and buy you a treat.* I used to wonder if this was performative but now I think it isn't, just a woman needing someone to listen to her thoughts. I never talked to Stella this way, never needed that kind of reflection from her. In this way I am lucky: I have my writing for that.

But even in this Stella was the best possible dog for me. If I arrived home irritated at having to leave an event early, or exhausted from teaching late into the night and grumpy from still needing to take her on a walk so she could "do her business," Stella never took it personally. All emotions but love rolled off her silky back. It's true that dogs love unconditionally, never hoping you'll change to be more like them, to see the world the way they do. This is one of the reasons I never confused Stella for human, never thought of her as one of my kids. My kids wished I was more like "other people's mothers," meaning, I suppose, more hovering and self-sacrificing, more sentimental and affectionate. My ex-husband wished I was more positive about the state of racial justice and equality in America, more willing to believe love conquered all. My family wished I wasn't a writer, or at least that I did not write about them or even about myself (because it reflected on them). A lot of people wished I would just stop talking. A lot of people wished I would no longer exist.

But Stella never wished me to be anything but what I was, at least not as far as I could tell, which is all that matters. She took me as I was. We had an understanding. We got along.

We kept Stella's bag of kibble right next to her eating spot but she never ripped it open, never knocked it down and ate what she wanted. She was sixty pounds in her prime, with teeth that shattered pork bones like they were crackers, chewed up rawhide like I chew gum. She could have killed us in our sleep but instead she begged for cheese when I was cooking. A wolf we let live in the house, who let us live. Such a strange relationship.

~

In 2012, a story appeared in the Chinese media of a mother bear, imprisoned with her cub on a "bile farm" (where bile is extracted from the gallbladders of caged animals for use in traditional Chinese medicines), who, hearing the distress cries of her cub one day, broke free, raced to her cub, smothered him to death and then ran into a wall, killing herself. I stumbled across the story years later, researching the suicide notes of famous writers for an essay, and was struck not so much by the notion than non-human animals might commit suicide as by the infanticide which proceeded the mother cub's death. Killing your own offspring to spare them a lifetime of cruelty and suffering is a powerful, impossible act of love. It reminded me of Toni Morrison's masterpiece *Beloved,* and of Harriet Jacob's famous narrative *Incidents in the Life of a Slave Girl.* It reminded me of slavery and the hard choices faced by enslaved Black women. It reminded me of us.

It never occurred to me to question what animals thought or did not think about death until Stella began to decline. It was slow but steady: a year, two years, three years. The three sets of stairs from the street to our old house set high on a hill, stairs she used to bound up and down, became a trial. Nuclear sclerosis clouded her vision; a cataract in one eye made her nearly blind. Her once-sharp hearing had diminished, her breath started to stink, she gained weight, had digestive problems, kept having

UTIs. Sometimes she wandered the house restlessly, barking at nothing, staring at doors. And she was in pain, that much was clear. She grew lethargic and listless and began to have such trouble moving around that I contacted the vet to ask about euthanasia. I was determined not to deny the inevitable, determined to be prepared.

But then, with a little help from modern pharmacology, Stella rallied. The vet put her on one medication for her arthritis, then, when that seemed to wane, added a second. We added CBD treats to the cocktail, hoping it would also soothe her dementia, calm her restlessness. By the end she was like my eighty-four-year-old mother, taking precise doses of multiple medicines several times a day. But eventually even those began to fail. She panted trying to rise in the morning, panted getting down the stairs. Some days she couldn't get comfortable. Her appetite waned. One day, practicing yoga in the living room, I looked up to find that she had defecated in the hallway. Stella had an accident, not even when (because of an emergency) she was left alone for fourteen hours. She was a camel. Until suddenly she was not. I put her gently outside and cleaned the house, then called her in. She looked up from her spot under the bushes but did not move. Was she ashamed? Dogs are intelligent, at least some of them (I have met, in my life, some very stupid dogs). Capable of complexities of behavior and levels of training that astonish us. But I am not a person who anthropomorphizes animals. Guilt and shame are human emotions; science tells us dogs only learn to "look" ashamed of themselves in reaction to their owner's anger or scolding. At worst, their actions indicate fear; at best, they are a bid to avoid scolding or punishment. I neither scolded nor punished Stella for shitting in the house, just let her sit outside beneath the bushes as long as she wanted. She wasn't, I think, ashamed of losing control of her bodily functions, not the way I would be. She was, I think, simply done.

But maybe that's also projection.

I texted my daughter in New York: *I think it's time.*

She texted back: *I'm coming home next week. Can you wait so I can be there?*

She was twenty-four at the time, becoming a social worker so her big heart could earn her living. Twenty-four and already willing to sit with the reality of death.

~

On the last day of Stella's life I gave her scrambled eggs with cheese for breakfast, as many CBD crackers as she wanted, ground beef for lunch. All day she sat at my feet while I tried to work, waiting for my daughter to arrive. When she did we took Stella for a slow walk around the neighborhood, letting her linger at every smell for as long as she liked. My husband came home early from work and we all sat around, waiting for the vet to arrive.

Stella was not a dog who hated going to the vet. For her, any ride in the car was a good ride, any experience in which people patted her back and snuck her treats a good experience. But I wanted her last moments to take place at home, so I scheduled an appointment with an amazing organization of veterinarians who will come to your house. It was strange, sitting in the living room on a beautiful July day, waiting for a woman to come and kill my dog.

When the doctor arrived she introduced herself, first to each of us and then to Stella, who sniffed her happily. The doctor sat on the floor with us and talked through the process, stressing that she would do nothing until we said so, that everything moved at our speed. The first step was a sedative to make Stella sleepy. The doctor took out a plastic cup full of peanut butter and I fed it to Stella while she gave her the shot. For what seemed like hours but was probably only twenty or thirty minutes we sat with Stella while she slipped into unconsciousness, petting her, stroking her, telling her what she had meant for our lives. We told stories about her shenanigans and laughed and rubbed her face and cried. The doctor made a clay paw print and took a tuft of hair. I don't know what to do with these things; I have yet to look at them.

When we were ready the doctor gently found a vein and injected the medicine that stopped Stella's heart. It happened quickly, the change from life to death. After maybe five minutes the vet lifted her stethoscope to listen. She said, "Stella's at peace." Saying a being who once lived and lives no longer is "at peace" is a euphemism, but I was grateful for it. It felt like truth.

~

Toward the end Stella had had good days and bad days and while it is true that the bad days had begun to outnumber the good there were still good days and in the last week of her life she'd had a spectacular one, eating heartily, flipping her paw over my arm when I rubbed her belly (her signature move but one which had dwindled), prancing instead of lumbering heavily on our daily constitution. I wavered. She might have another week, another month, another three months with some days good and some days bad. What's the ratio of good to bad that tips the balance? Who decides? Who has the right?

I know a man who believed he did not. His aging dog grew so infirm he found her every morning covered in shit. When it got to the point they couldn't even clean her anymore because her hind quarters had atrophied so much, the maggots came. Still he refused until one day the dog's heart finally faltered. Was this more humane? Was this a better death? Or is that besides the point? For a year I contemplated the death of Stella, wondering less about right, more about responsibility.

I don't know whether or not it was the right thing to do. It was the thing I did; it was the thing I would do again. It was terrible and beautiful and moving. It was the thing I want someone to do for me when my time comes, and if Stella taught me anything it is that my time, like yours, is coming. Isn't the real gift of pets not their love and companionship but the way their abbreviated lifes forces us to confront the reality of death? And the importance of quality, not simply quantity?

Or maybe I'm projecting.

I thought I was prepared for Stella's death. I thought I would be sad but not devastated; it makes no sense, I thought, to be devastated by the death of a pet, to be shocked by the passing of an animal you knew would only live so long. Wasn't that just the result of denial, of avoiding the truth of one's own looming mortality? A woman I know, trying for comfort, cried out at the news of Stella's passing, saying: "Oh my God! Losing a dog is the worst!"

No, I thought, not the worst. So many worse things can happen. So many worse things will.

Another woman told me she took to her bed for three days when her dog died. I did not take to my bed after the vet took Stella's body away. I just cried. Then we ordered dinner and went to sleep and got up and went to a wedding. Later I cried again. I'm crying now.

People say "We don't deserve dogs." This much is true but still I hate when people say it; it's sentimental and sentimentality is a way of people in the world that lets people off the hook. Sentimental people stare out at society through sunshine glasses, which is great for them but does very little for change. Sentimentality is a dishonest glossing over, an avoidance of life and its messiness. Like people who shrug and say "I'm a hopeless romantic" to explain the disastrous decisions they make and keep on making about love. How odd to celebrate hopelessness, to revel in intentional incompetence. I'm hopeless at basketball, mostly because I've never tried to get better. I don't go around bragging about it.

I didn't deserve Stella but then again I haven't deserved most of the things I've been given in life, most of the challenges and most of the blessings, most of the tribulations and most of the gifts. Almost no one, for better or worse, gets what they really deserve in life. Deserving has very little to do with anything.

We don't deserve dogs, which is a minor tribute to them and a far harsher condemnation of us. After all, dogs love us because we bred them to do so. It takes between six and eight generations to domesticate a canine, six or seven or eight lifetimes of wooing and rewarding and bribery.[5] Left to itself the wolf, like most intelligent animals, wants nothing to do with humanity. We breed them to adore us and then feel good about ourselves when the adoration comes. We breed them to love us and then make very little effort to live up to that love, to be the benevolent gods we have made ourselves

---

5. Jacobson, Lindsey. "Review of The History of Dogs as Pets." ABC News. August 26, 2016. https://abcnews.go.com/Lifestyle/history-dogs-pets/story?id=41671149.

in their eyes. Lavishing your dog with expensive treats and anthropomorphizing attention doesn't make you a good person; even Hitler loved his animals.

We don't deserve dogs and dogs are probably part of the reason for that discrepancy. Dogs let us off the hook.

I didn't deserve Stella but there she was anyway. For a time.

Gimme a Head with Hair

The longest, most ambivalent (in the true sense of the word) and most complex relationship of my life, outside of the mother–daughter connection, has been with my hair. For Black women, this is not unusual.

It began off-balance; my hair loved me but I didn't love it back. I yearned for hair of a different kind. Like many little Black girls in America, especially chubby little Black girls, especially chubby little Black girls coming of age in the 1970s and 1980s, I took my cues on what was beautiful and desirable mostly from television. (I say mostly but not entirely: there was plenty of internalized racism floating around, and my skin was not "light" and my hair was not "good" and I was also strangely and awkwardly tall though I did have what my uncle used to call, confusingly, "big damn eyes.") On TV, beauty was Mary Tyler Moore and Angie Dickinson and Lindsey Wagner and Peggy Lipton ("one Black, one White, one blonde," as if blonde were its own separate race, which I guess it kinda is) and Jaclyn Smith and, especially, Farrah—who was, unlike most celebrated American blondes, genuinely beautiful.

Black women were, for the most part, maternal and long-suffering and strong, or maybe snarky and wisecracking and forever just passing through the room. Isabel Sanford and Marla Gibbs and Ester Rolle (and Ja'Net DuBois and Bernadette Stanis, but they were rarely center stage) and Danielle Spencer and Mabel King, all extraordinary actors (especially Rolle) of great presence and power, but they hardly ever got the flowers and almost never got the guy. Unless the guy was George Jefferson.

All of which is to say that during those years when self-identity is formed, I, like many Black girls, thought myself ugly. In some ways, this turned out to be more blessing than curse; believing one must rely on something other than one's face and one's ass to get through the world is not the worst thing that can happen to a girl. I thought that I would have to rely upon my brain and I was glad it was good and I worked to make it better and my brain pushed me along. That foundation has made seeing those first gray hairs and deepening lines in the forehead a little easier. (Make no mistake: all those bikini pictures of aging actresses and models on Instagram are acts not of confidence or affirmation, but of panic.)

Still, there's no denying the pain of measuring oneself "by the tape of a world that looks on in amused contempt and pity," as W.E.B. DuBois famously wrote in *The Souls of Black Folk*. It's easy for me to mock these gargantuan pickup trucks that seem to have taken over three-quarters of the male population in America, easy for me to mock the cosplay of the Harley-Davidson guys—freedom, independence and rugged individuality, mass-produced and neatly packaged. It's easy for me to mock how men invest so much in these external markers of identity because I don't care about trucks or fishing poles or bikes. They don't make me feel any certain way, but my hair does. My hair is me. Or so I always thought.

～

Not being able to change my skin to win society's approval, I changed my hair. For years I hot-combed, relaxed and jheri curled, sponge-rolled, straightened and weaved. Even when I was not actively tending, processing or reshaping my hair, I worried about it. Rolling every night, brushing out every morning, counting the broken hairs in the sink. All damn day Saturday in the beauty shop. Those years when I paid good money to have somebody else's hair sewn into mine so that I could swing a ponytail, and if anyone dared question I would put my hands on my hips in false bravado and retort, "Yes, it's mine. I paid for it."

It's strange how we cling to dead things.

When I became pregnant with my first child, it finally dawned on me to wonder what slathering lye on my scalp every four to six weeks was doing to my insides—and what it might do to the fetus I was carrying. I'd given up alcohol, caffeine and pumping my own gas; was I still going to spend time in the beauty shop passively ingesting chemicals and paying for the privilege?

I was not.

I chopped it off.

For maybe six months I wore a short afro, the first time in my life I allowed my hair to be as it was. It was strangely, sadly difficult. Many people complimented me; my husband said he liked it. I was the only one who was uncomfortable. My sisters and mother were still all relaxing their hair, as were most of my girlfriends. I felt unattractive, unfeminine and alone. The wounds of anti-Blackness cut pretty deep.

When my hair was long enough again, I turned to braids. For only $200 (or whatever; I can't remember the cost but it was a lot), six or eight hours of your life and a headache that will last a week you too can have long, swinging hair. Wearing braids was like a courtship with my hair, a step toward real and lasting love. But you can't keep dating forever (I mean, you can but what's the point?) A relationship is like a mako shark (not all sharks!): it has to keep moving or it dies.

So I decided to loc my hair. It felt like a big decision, bigger even than cutting off my relaxed tresses. People warned: "Once you do it, you won't be able to go back. You'll have to cut all your hair off all over again."

Like most things people say, this turned out to not be strictly true. After nearly twenty years of wedded bliss, years in which I grew to finally love the stuff coming out of my head the way it loves me, I decided to untangle my locs. All it took was a ton of conditioner, tireless arms and a week off from work.

⮿

Today, I face the final frontier in hair self-acceptance: going gray. This one is hard for everyone.

"Ditching the dye," said Ronnie Citron-Fink, who wrote a book about the dangers of denying Mother Nature's hint, "would mean confronting strongly held cultural beliefs . . . some so ingrained, I was barely aware of them: about beauty, choice, aging, and femininity. It would also mean flouting fashion and beauty gurus, the media, decades of powerful and seductive advertising, my girlfriends, even the expectations of the men in my life."

In youth-worshiping America, going gray is a big decision for any woman. Note how Mitch McConnell can wield power and Bernie Sanders can run for president with heads full of white hair but Nancy Pelosi and Elizabeth Warren have to maintain an air of youthfulness, or at least middle-agedness.

As with many things, women pay a higher price for maintaining this perception of youthfulness—and Black women pay perhaps the highest price of all. Research on the dangers of hair dye is limited (a gendered reality in and of itself) and conflicting, but some of the more than 5,000 chemicals used in hair dyes are known carcinogens. Moreover, scientists at the National Institute of Health have recently found that women who use permanent hair dyes and chemical straighteners have a higher risk of breast cancer than women who don't.

For African American women, using permanent dyes every five to eight weeks or more was associated with a 60 percent increased risk of breast cancer as compared with an 8 percent increased risk for White women.

Sixty percent.

A few years ago I largely switched from chemical dyes to henna to cover those scary gray hairs sprouting around my face. But applying henna correctly takes hours, and after two decades of (essentially) carefree locs, I struggle with the patience required to spend time mixing and heating and waiting and rinsing and washing and doing it again.

The truth is that my hair is telling me that going gray is the next, necessary step in our relationship. I will admit that it is scary. My mother says, "Aging is not for wimps."

But I have learned to always listen to my hair.

A Talk to Students

I should begin by telling you that I have walked out on commencement speakers more than once in my life, so I won't take it personally if you get up and go for water during these brief remarks. The first time I walked out was at my own college graduation; a group of maybe twenty or twenty-five of us talked for weeks about staging a protest by standing up and marching out of the stadium when the guest speaker, Lee Ioccoa, began to speak. In the end, whether from disorganization, fear or sheer laziness, we ended up, at the critical moment, just kind of turning our backs. It looked like we were rearranging our gowns; no one noticed the protest at all, especially not Lee Ioccoa. I remember nothing he said that day, or even why we were protesting him. He was, in the end, no better or worse than any other capitalist.

I did actually walk out on the speaker at my daughter's high school graduation, afraid that if I didn't leave I would stand up and call the man a racist, which he most certainly was. This wouldn't have bothered me but I feared it might embarrass my child. I also walked out on the speaker at my stepdaughter's college commencement, the then-governor of Massachusetts.

He was admonishing the graduates—many of them immigrants, Black and Latino, first-generation college attendees—to simply work hard and "make good decisions" like his grandparents had done and the American dream would surely be theirs. This from a wealthy White man whose father, grandfather and great grandfather were all prominent politicians, well-established and well-funded in their time. The oblivious finger-wagging incensed me; I had to leave the stadium to keep from blowing my top. But on the way out I noticed no one else was angry because no one was listening.

That nobody listens to graduation speeches may be the saving grace of the bulk of them. Between myself, my siblings, my children and stepchildren and nearly three decades of teaching I must have sat through probably fifty graduation and commencement speeches, some of them by prominent and even famous people. I don't remember a word.

We rarely listen to advice even when we ask for it, which helps to explain the exceptionally slow pace of human emotional and psychological development. If we proceeded with our technology the way we proceed with understanding how humans work, every generation would have to start by inventing the internal combustion engine, learning through trial and error how to make wagons go fast without the use of a horse. Life, as they say, is a tough teacher: she gives you the test first and the lesson afterward. This is terrible pedagogy.

Regardless, it is the task of a commencement speaker to

offer advice, so here I go. I'm going to begin with a theory, one which, at first, may seem to have little to do with the reason we are gathered today. I want to tell you about the neighborhood where I live, a great place. And one of the reasons it's great (and the reason I chose it) is the diversity. It's not a nirvana—no place is, especially around Boston—but in terms of racial, ethnic, gender and orientation diversity, we're pretty good. There are Black folks, White folks, Asian and Latinx folks (from all over the Latin American diaspora.) There are LGBTQ folks and many immigrants and people whose families have lived in and around Boston since the Civil War. There are renters and homeowners and some low-income housing and more than a few million dollar homes. There are old people and many young couples, and people like me, who are in-between. It's great. But in nearly three decades in my neighborhood something I had seen only once was a White family with adopted Black children, and in that case, the children were actually biracial. But a few months ago I noticed that I was seeing more and more such families: young White couples strolling the sidewalks and playing at the park with adopted Black kids. I counted at least four such families around the neighborhood. And all the children were boys.

I have a theory about this. It's a theory because as a writer, a former journalist and an educator I know not to leap from observation to conclusion. I know I need to not only "do my own research" but to critically evaluate that research, assessing the sources and testing its validity before integrating it into my knowledge base. Since I haven't done that, what I'm about to tell you remains a theory. Proceed accordingly.

I think what I am observing in my little corner of the world is what I dubbed the "This Is Us" effect. Now, in case you've been in seclusion, *This Is Us* was a hugely popular American television show which aired between 2016 and 2022. It was about a White family with two biological children and an adopted Black son, all who happened to have been born on the same day at the same hospital. Naturally this unique family undergoes all kinds of trials and tribulations but everyone is quirky and attractive and accomplished and in the end they all love each other more than anything and there is always sentimental music playing in the background to make you cry.

If my theory is correct—if this television show about a loving White family with an adopted Black son spurred an increase in the number of actual White families adopting Black children— then what this theory makes vivid is the astonishing power of narrative, of storytelling and communication and the Word. I'm not going to get into the pros and cons of interracial adoption— that's another discussion. I will not even here give you my critique of the truthfulness of this glossy Hollywood product, the ways it did or did not confront the complicated reality of Black children raised by White parents in a White supremacist society. I won't give that critique because I don't want to stray too far from my point and also because it wouldn't be fair: the show annoyed me so much I stopped watching after the first year. What I'm focusing on today is the impact we, as artists and communicators, can have on the world.

Among the buzz words whirring around higher education currently is creativity. A liberal arts education, we are told, nurtures critical thinking skills, innovation, creativity. All of this is true, without question. But creativity itself is neutral. It can be used to enlighten or deceive, to unite or divide, to construct or destroy. You want to know who was creative? David Wark Griffith, who pioneered many aspects of filmmaking and film editing, doing things with a camera no one had done before. Likewise Leni Riefenstahl, another person who was creative as hell. Creativity is not inherently good. You must make a choice to use it for such.

My vision for higher education is to unleash upon the world a tsunami of people who will be creative forces for good. For compassion and liberation and the construction of a just and equitable society. I believe our grad programs are training not only top-notch journalists and filmmakers and writers and communication professionals and publishers and speech language pathologists and theater educators and marketers and creative entrepreneurs—but the next generation of leaders in these fields. People who will not only *be* the change, but will lead it. More than ever, the world is in desperate need of such leaders. To say these past few years of pandemic and economic instability and rising inequality and political strife and what some people have called a racial reckoning—though I suspect it is really just another turn in the cycle of progress and backlash that is American history—to say all this has been challenging would be an understatement. These are, without question, hard times.

But Toni Morrison said that hard times are precisely the times when artists go to work. Hard times are when artists and journalists and scholars and teachers of every kind go to work. That was the original meaning of a master's degree, you know, a declaration that a person admitted to the rank of "master" or teacher, at one university should also be admitted to the same rank at other universities. Now that you are a "master" you have the right to call yourself an expert in your field, but you also have an obligation to do something with that expertise, something that extends beyond yourself. We're big on rights in this country and that's all well and good but the flip side of a right is a duty. A society built on rights without duty is like a skyscraper without a foundation. It might look pretty. But it won't stand for long.

A society depends on community. *Merriam Webster* defines community as a "unified body of individuals." In America we tend to take that definition backward, starting with "individuals"— and stubbornly halting there. Individuality is important. But community requires a *unified* body of individuals, organized, the dictionary says, for some purpose. Unity and purpose are where we get stuck.

Unity does not mean groupthink. Unity does not mean

an erasure of difference. Audre Lorde said, "difference must be not merely tolerated, but seen as a fund of necessary polarities between which our creativity can spark like a dialectic. Only then does the necessity for interdependency become unthreatening." In other words, we're all in this boat together. Either we row together, or we row individually and, at best, we'll go in circles and, more likely, we'll go down. It really is that simple, and that true.

During your time here you will learn and grow and connect, and you will also disagree. With a classmate or a professor or a staff member. Perhaps, in this disagreement, you will think yourself *wronged.* Perhaps you will be certain that you are, in fact, right. I used to put great stock in being right, until someone asked me, "Do you want to be right? Or do you want to be loved?" When you disagree with that classmate or professor or staff member, I hope you'll ask yourself: "Do I want to be right, or do I want to be in community?"

I want to be *in* community. That doesn't mean swallowing my opinion or not speaking up or not challenging things I think wrong. It means doing those things in a way that respects not only the human being on the other side but also the reality of our interdependence. Failing that acknowledgement, we are lost. We cannot allow ourselves to be lost. There must always be hope.

There must also be healing. And I'm sorry but your generation is going to have to do it. We tried. I know it doesn't look like it but we did. Sometimes it was two steps forward and three steps back but we did our best and we accomplished some things. Apartheid. Gay marriage. The bald eagle! And seat belts. When I was a kid nobody wore seat belts. My mother would pile us kids onto the front bench seat of the car and take off down the road without a second thought. If she had to stop short she'd stick out her arm to keep us from flying through the windshield. I remember when seat belt use became mandatory. People pitched a fit. My Uncle Jesse said a seat belt ruined the crease of his pants and nobody and nothing was gonna make him buckle up in his own car. Then an accident left another uncle paralyzed, and everybody in the family came around. Today seat belt use hovers around 90 percent. Seat belts save about 15,000 lives a year. Things can change.

But although change is inevitable, progress is not. Maybe you've heard the phrase "the arc of the moral universe is long but it bends toward justice." This is Dr. Martin Luther King's eloquent restatement of a line from nineteenth century minister and abolitionist Theodore Parker. Reverend Parker's sermon is more ambiguous than King's restatement, which itself, in full context, is actually more ambiguous than the line we often hear. Always read the whole speech. Parker said, "I do not pretend to understand the moral universe; the arc is a long one, my eye reaches but little ways; I cannot calculate the curve and complete the figure by the experience of sight; I can divine it by conscience. And from what I see I am sure it bends toward justice."

Well. Lord knows I don't understand the moral universe either. And far be it for me to contradict either Reverend Parker or Dr. King. But *from what I* see, what I have seen, the arc of the moral universe bends whichever way it gets pulled. The forces bending it toward inequity and injustice, toward war and climate disaster and authoritarianism—these are powerful forces. Endlessly strong. The only way to counter them is with collective effort. The only way to bend the arc back the other way is for each and every one of us to grab hold and pull. Hard.

The good news is this: if we have done our jobs, and I hope we have, then you've spent the past few years here building up your muscles. Your professors gave you some eight-pound free weights or maybe some twenty-pound ones if you actually took a philosophy class. The experiences you shared with faculty and classmates were resistance bands. Living through a pandemic, seeing both the worst and the best of humankind—this has been one big kettlebell. You've been working out hard these past few years and now you leave pumped up and ready to grab hold of that arc and bend it the way it must be bent if we are to thrive, not only as a society, not only as a nation, but as human beings in the full sense of that word.

James Baldwin said not to be fooled when looking at the enormity of the problems compared to the small number of people determined to set things right. A majority, he said, had nothing to do with numbers. It has to do with influence. "The majority for which everyone is seeking, which must reassess and release us from our past and deal with the present and create standards worthy of what a man may be—this majority is you. No one else can do it. The world is before you and you need not take it or leave it as it was when you came in."

Periracial

When a White person says he or she is sick and tired of hearing or thinking or talking about race, I want to cackle and caw and roll on the floor shrieking with hysterical, life-altering laughter, and also to haul my aging bones to the nearest window, crank it open, climb to the sill while unfurling my homemade blue wings like a character in a Toni Morrison novel and just . . . leap. I want to do these things because the statement is just that funny and just that absurd and just that obscene and just that ridiculous and just that maddening. You're sick and tired of hearing about race? *You're* sick and tired of hearing and talking and thinking about race? Hahahahahahahahah!

How the fuck do you think we feel?

Imagine this. You live in a building, a big building, vast and imposing and somewhat grand if also a bit inelegant. Imagine you live on the bottom floor, where the pipes leak and the concrete chips and the garbage sometimes piles in the hall and sometimes you protest but for the most part you and your people live with it because it is what it is and anyway what choice do you have? The higher floors are nicer, you know that much; no rats running around up there. Maybe you'll get up there some day, but, in the meantime you just live.

Imagine one day when you're fourteen or fifteen you go into the basement and discover that the foundation is rotting, crumbling like a termite-infested stump. You're not the only one who sees this; an old man from your floor tells you it's been that way as long as he's lived. An old woman says it's been that way from the beginning, that from the start the foundation was bound to deteriorate because it was made of cardboard and cigarettes, of tobacco and sugar cane, of hair and teeth and blood and bones. You start trying to alert people to this problem. Many of the people on your floor know about the problem; many, but not all. Some shrug it off, some focus on moving higher, some have tried to do something or at least warn all those above. But the higher up you go in the building, the more people either ignore or deny the problem.

You spend the next forty-odd years of your life talking about the foundation, believing that if the people above knew what was happening, they'd surely do something, if not for the sake of the people on the bottom floors, at least for themselves. You talk and talk and talk, but every conversation is like starting all over again. *What are you talking about? What foundation? What do you mean?* Even people on the midlevel floor on which you now live get sick of hearing about the foundation eventually. Can't you talk about anything else?

When you visit the top almost nobody wants to hear about the rotten foundation. They say you're imagining it or flat-out lying, that you're either bitter or scamming, or possibly insane. Not everything is about the foundation. They refuse to even go look at the problem, let alone try to fix it. They're too busy adding on floors, using materials they've stolen from below. They're too busy redecorating the living room.

It's a weak metaphor but I can't think of a better one. I'm too tired.

⌁

I was born in Memphis in 1964 (year of the landmark Civil Rights Act), and grew up in that bluesy, beaten, beautiful southern city during the 1970s. When I mention these facts to my students, most of whom have grown up in the Northeast or the Mid-Atlantic or on the West Coast, they brace themselves for stories of violent racism, of pot-bellied sheriffs and skin-ripping dogs. When I tell them that, contrary to their imaginations, the Memphis of my childhood was collaborative and calm, they don't believe me. When I tell them Black kids and White kids mixed easily from my first day of kindergarten, that my elementary and middle schools were almost certainly more integrated than their own, their mouths fall open. When I tell these students that for the first fifteen or so years of my life race was a fact but not an issue, that I came of age with a sense of hopefulness and progress, that not only did I believe, as a child, that things were getting better, they actually were—they are shocked.

"What happened?" they ask.

"What always happens," I say. "Backlash."

Looking back over my sixty years of this American life, I see three cycles of progress and backlash. The first began before my birth and ended in 1980 with the election of You-Know-Who. Progress of a relative, truncated kind began again with Bill Clinton and ended with the backlash election of affable-but-deadly George W. Bush. Progress—more than we had quite believed possible, less, in retrospect, than it seemed at the time—with the election of You-Definitely-Know-Who in 2008, ending in the backlash-to-end-all-backlashes in 2017.

So far anyway.

I cried when Ronald Reagan was elected president, knowing, as I did, what it meant for poor people and Black people (though not what it meant to democracy and the middle-class and the environment.) When Baby Bush was elected I cried, though not as hard, knowing what it meant for Black people and poor people (though not what it meant for one million Iraqis, American Muslims or the US economy.) When Trump was running and people said there was just no way a man like that could ever be elected president of the United States, I asked if they meant this United States. When he was elected I cursed and spat and deflated and cursed some more. I did not cry. To quote Baby

Bush: Fool me once, shame on you. Fool me twice . . . you can't get fooled again.

·~

Peri. From Ancient Greek. As a prefix meaning around or surrounding, as in perimeter; near, as in perihelion; or during, as in perinatal. In Persian folklore, peri is a supernatural being descended from fallen angels and excluded from paradise until penance is accomplished. In Finnish the prefix *peri* means *very*, or *to the core*, making *perikato* mean utter ruin or destruction. *Rasismin vie tämän maan perikatoon.* Racism will be the undoing of this country / will lead this country into ruin.

Isn't language fun?

Looking back I can see that I used to believe that writing and speaking and teaching and talking about all this stuff would make a difference. Would wake people up from their slumber of White innocence and lead them to action. I used to believe that my voice could join the chorus of voices far, far greater than mine, stretching back to Walker and Jacobs and Douglass and Harper and upward through DuBois and Hurston and Wright and Wells and Baldwin and hooks and on and on and help move the needle forward, help tip the boulder over the edge. I used to believe America— stubborn, resistant, willfully innocent America—could grow up and be better than it had been before. I must have believed all that, though now it seems unlikely. Why else would I have bothered all these years?

Bitterness is a potential hazard of advancing years. So is nostalgia. So is delusion. So is sentimentality.

What does periracial mean? Who knows? It's a word I made up while casting about for a way to capture both the chronic nature of structural injustice and inequity of America and my own weariness. A way to label life under that particular tooth in the zipper of interlocking systems of oppression bell hooks called "imperialist White supremacist capitalist heteropatriarchy." (What a lot to resist. No wonder we're so tired!) To capture the endless cycle of progress and backlash which has shaped my one small life here in America during the end of the twentieth century and the first part of the twenty-first. To counter the idea—now largely abandoned but innocently believed for most of my adult life by White Americans on both ends of the political spectrum—that America has ever been postracial.

To suggest that I suspect, at this sad rate, we never will be.

Acknowledgments

Writing is a solitary act, but living is a communal one. With deep gratitude I would like to acknowledge all the people in my community without whom my life, and thus this book, would not be possible. My mother, who started it all. My three sisters and baby brother, who have always been along for the ride. My friends in Boston and around the country, and the world. My colleagues at Emerson College and the neighbors in my neighborhood. My children Samantha and Isaac. Robert and Elizabeth, of Ig Publishing, where I have found a home. And Ray.

Works Cited

"Antisocial Personality Disorder." Mayo Clinic, February 24, 2023. https://www.mayoclinic.org/diseases-conditions/antisocial-personality-disorder/symptoms-causes/syc-20353928.

Ayeni, Tofe. "Ghana: Did the 'Year of Return' Manage to Import the Capital, Skills and Diaspora It Promised?" *The Africa Report*, February 22, 2022. https://www.theafricareport.com/178482/ghana-did-the-year-of-return-manage-to-import-the-capital-skills-and-diaspora-it-promised/.

Bell, Derrick. "Racism Is Here to Stay: Now What." *Howard Law Review* 35, no. 1 (1991): 79–93.

Del Toro, Juan, and Ming- Te Wang. "The Longitudinal Inter-Relations Between School Discipline and Academic Performance: Examining the Role of School Climate." *American Psychologist*, September 2021.

Douglass, Frederick. *Narrative of the life of Frederick Douglass, an American slave, written by himself.* Edited by John R. McKivigan, Peter P. Hinks, and Heather L. Kaufman. New Haven: Yale University Press, 2016.

Gilchrist, Elizabeth. "The Cognition of Domestic Abusers: Explanations, Evidence and Treatment." Essay. In *Aggressive Offenders' Cognition: Theory, Research, and Practice*, edited by

Theresa A. Gannon, Tony Ward, Anthony R. Beech, and Dawn Fisher, 247–66. New York: Wiley-Interscience, 2007. https://onlinelibrary.wiley.com/doi/book/10.1002/9780470746295.

Graham, G.R. *Graham's American Monthly Magazine of Literature, Art, And Fashion.* 42, 1853 January-June. Philadelphia. Accessed: Hathi Trust Digital Library.

Hill, Jess. "It's Like You Go to Abuse School: How Domestic Violence Always Follows the Same Script." *The Guardian,* June 23, 2019. https://www.theguardian.com/society/2019/jun/24/its-like-you-go-to-abuse-school-how-domestic-violence-always-follows-the-same-script

hooks, bell. *Communion: The female search for love.* London: Perennial, 2021.

Hughey, Matthew W. "Debating Du Bois's Darkwater: From Hymn of Hate to Pathos and Power." *Identities Global Studies in Culture and Power,* 2020. https://www.academia.edu/43034547/_Debating_Du_Boiss_Darkwater_From_hymn_of_hate_to_pathos_and_power_.

"Inventing Black and White." Facing History and Ourselves, August 11, 2017. https://www.facinghistory.org/resource-library/inventing-black-white.

"Let's talk about black americans and stroke," 2019. https://www.stroke.org/-/media/Stroke-Files/Lets-Talk-About-Stroke/Prevention/Lets-Talk-About-Black-Americans-and-Stroke-Sheet.pdf.

Kamin, Debra. "Widespread Racial Bias Found in Home Appraisals." *The New York Times,* November 2, 2022. https://www.nytimes.com/2022/11/02/realestate/racial-bias-home-appraisals.html

McGoogan, Cara. "'You're a Slave': Inside Louisiana's Forced Prison Labor and a Failed Overhaul Attempt." *The Washington Post*, January 1, 2023. https://www.washingtonpost.com/ nation/2023/01/01/louisiana-prison-labor-ballot-slavery/.

Romano, Aja. "A History of 'Wokeness.'" *Vox*, October 9, 2020. https://www.vox.com/culture/21437879/stay-woke-woke-ness-history-origin-evolution-controversy.

Schenwar, Maya. "Slavery Haunts America's Plantation Prisons." *Prison Legal News*, April 15, 2009. https://www.prisonlegal-news.org/news/2009/apr/15/slavery-haunts-americas-plantation-prisons-by-maya-schenwar/.

"Stroke and African Americans." Office of Minority Health (OMH). https://minorityhealth.hhs.gov/omh/browse.aspx-?lvl=4&lvlid=28.

The Liberator. William Lloyd Garrison, publisher.

Tiku, Nitasha. "Google's Plan to Talk about Caste Bias Led to 'Division and Rancor.'" *The Washington Post*, June 2, 2022. https://www.washingtonpost.com/technology/2022/06/02/ google-caste-equality-labs-tanuja-gupta/.

Walker, David. *Walker's Appeal, in Four Articles; Together with a Preamble, to the Coloured Citizens of the World, but in Particular, and Very Expressly, to Those of the United States of America, Written in Boston, State of Massachusetts*, September 28, 1829. https://docsouth.unc.edu/nc/walker/walker.html

Yearby, Ruqaiijah, Brietta Clark, and José F. Figueroa. "Structural Racism In Historical And Modern US Health Care Policy." *Health Affairs* 41, no. 2 (February 2022). https://www. healthaffairs.org/doi/full/10.1377/hlthaff.2021.01466.